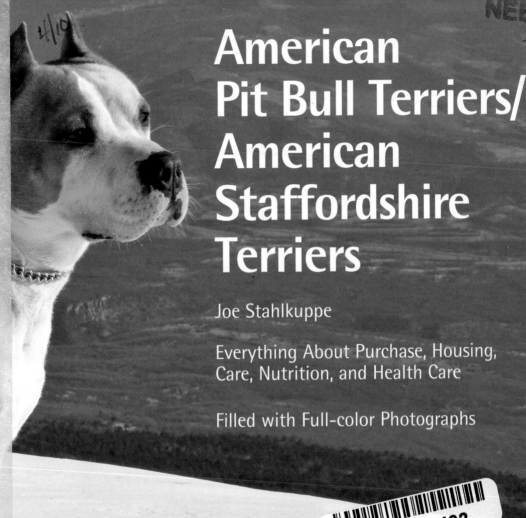

# American Pit Bull Terriers/ American Staffordshire Terriers

Joe Stahlkuppe

Everything About Purchase, Housing, Care, Nutrition, and Health Care

Filled with Full-color Photographs

BARRON'S

W9-AMT-402

**Brief History** 5

The Common
Misperception 5

The Fighting Dog Heritage 6

Their Recent Bad
Reputation and
How It Happened 6

Human Culprits 6

A Canine Loose Cannon? 8

**Should You Own an
APBT/Amstaff Terrier?** 11

Basic Dog Owner
Responsibilities 11

Additional APBT/Amstaff
Owner Responsibilities 11

A Male or a Female? 12

A Puppy or an Older Dog? 12

An APBT or an Amstaff? 13

**The Adoption Option** 17

Effect and Cause 17

The Answer 18

Concerns 18

Outcome 19

**Considerations Before
Buying/Adopting** 21

What You Should Expect 21

Guarantees 23

Selecting the Right Puppy 24

Selecting the Right
Shelter/Rescue Animal 25

Before You Bring Your
APBT/Amstaff Home 25

HOW-TO: Puppy Proofing 28

**Bringing Your APBT/
Amstaff Terrier Home** 31

First Things First 31

Socialization 31

Adjustment Time 33

The Cage/Crate/Carrier 34

Helping Your Puppy
Settle In 37

The Crucial Early Lessons 38

636.7559 STA
1550 6093 4-7-2010 NEB
Stahlkuppe, Joe.

American pit bull
terriers/American
KGW

LeRoy Collins Leon County
**PUBLIC LIBRARY SYSTEM**
200 West Park Avenue
Tallahassee, Florida 32301-7720

## A Word About Pronouns

Many APBT/Amstaff owners feel that the pronoun "it" is not appropriate when referring to a pet that can be such a wonderful part of our lives. For this reason, APBT/ Amstaff Terriers are referred to as "Bruiser" or "he" in this book unless the topic specifically relates to female dogs. No gender bias is intended by this writing style.

## About the Author

Joe Stahlkuppe is a widely read pet columnist, author, and freelance feature writer. He works as the Community Affairs Director for *HumaneSocietyAdoptions.com*, an international online company that helps homeless pets find homes and petless people find pets.

## Acknowledgments

This book is dedicated to Cesar Milan and his wonderful American Pit Bull Terrier, Daddy. I also want to express my deepest appreciation to Barron's Associate Editor, Angela Tartaro, without whom this book would be just a jumble of phrases and photographs.

The outstanding rescue work done by Pit Bull Rescue Central (PBRC) and the Staffordshire Club of America Rescue Committee must be highly commended. Also worthy of praise is Bama Bully Rescue—they do so much with a very limited budget.

My wife, Cathie, my son, Shawn, and my grandchildren, Catie, Peter, Julia, and Alexandra have all been strong supporters of my interest in dogs. I also want to thank and acknowledge the Vietnam veterans in the PTSD group at the Veteran's Medical Center in Birmingham, Alabama.

**Cover Photos**

Shutterstock: front cover, back cover, inside front cover, inside back cover.

**Photo Credits**

Kent Dannen: pages 7, 10, 15; Isabelle Francais: pages 2–3, 4, 8, 11, 13, 14, 16, 17, 18, 19, 20, 21, 27, 32, 35, 36, 40, 48, 49, 50, 57, 59, 60, 62, 63, 64, 66, 67, 69, 73, 74, 77, 78, 81; Oliver Lucanus: pages 44, 46, 47, 68; Paulette Johnson: pages 9, 22, 30, 31, 37, 38, 39, 45, 54, 58, 61, 65, 72, 82, 87, 88, 89, 90; Pet Profiles: pages 23, 84; Pets by Paulette: pages 5, 24, 41, 43, 51, 52, 55; Connie Summers/Paulette Johnson: pages 26, 33, 34, 42, 52, 75; Bruce Everett Webb: pages 12, 56, 93.

© Copyright 2010, 2000 by Barron's Educational Series, Inc.

All rights reserved.
No part of this book may be reproduced or distributed in any form or by any means without the written permission of the copyright owner.

*All inquiries should be addressed to:*
Barron's Educational Series, Inc.
250 Wireless Boulevard
Hauppauge, NY 11788
**www.barronseduc.com**

ISBN-13: 978-0-7641-4322-9
ISBN-10: 0-7641-4322-0

*Library of Congress Catalog Card No. 2009039853*

**Library of Congress Cataloging-in-Publication Data**
Stahlkuppe, Joe.
American pit bull terriers/American Staffordshire terriers : everything about purchase, housing, care, nutrition, behavior, and training / Joe Stahlkuppe.
  p. cm. — (A complete pet owner's manual)
  Includes index.
  ISBN-13: 978-0-7641-4322-9
  ISBN-10: 0-7641-4322-0
  1. American pit bull terrier. 2. American Staffordshire terrier. I. Title.
  SF429.A72S72 2010
  636.755'9—dc22                    2009039853

Printed in China
9 8 7 6 5 4 3 2 1

## Understanding Your APBT/Amstaff Terrier 41

The APBT/Amstaff as a Canine Companion 41

The APBT/Amstaff and Children 42

The APBT/Amstaff and Other Dogs 44

The APBT/Amstaff and Other Pets 45

The APBT/Amstaff and Guests in the Home 45

The APBT/Amstaff and Strangers 45

The APBT/Amstaff in the Neighborhood 46

## Caring for Your APBT/Amstaff Terrier 49

Keeping Your APBT/Amstaff Out of Bad Spots 49

Exercise 50

Grooming 50

Feeding 51

Housetraining 52

## Training Your APBT/Amstaff Terrier 55

Special Considerations for APBT/Amstaff Training 55

Training an Adopted Adult Dog 55

Pack Behavior and Your APBT/Amstaff 56

Build on the Mother Dog's Training Model 57

How Dog Training Works 58

Crate Training 58

Basic Training 60

The Essentials of Training Your Puppy 61

The Right Training Equipment 63

The Five Basic Commands 63

Obedience Classes to Help You *AND* Your Dog 69

HOW-TO: Housetraining 70

## Medical Care 73

Developing a Wellness Plan for Your Pet 73

A Health Care Team 73

Preventing Accidents 74

Preventing Illnesses 74

Immunizations 74

Common Ailments in the APBT/Amstaff 75

Other Possible Health Problems 78

Parasites 81

Emergency Care 85

Checklist: Helping an Injured Pet 86

Areas Requiring Lifelong Attention 87

Administering Medicine 90

When Your APBT/Amstaff Grows Older 91

## Information 92

Index 94

# BRIEF HISTORY

*Over the last three decades, no breed of dog has been more maligned and misunderstood than the American Pit Bull Terrier (APBT) and its close kin, the American Staffordshire Terrier. Much of this negativity is based on myth, hype, and ignorance.*

There is no real breed named "pit bull." Several breeds, the American Pit Bull Terrier, the American Staffordshire Terrier, the Staffordshire Bull Terrier, the Bull Terrier, and a dozen others and mixes of these dogs have all been scarred by this hateful brand.

## The Common Misperception

Just the mention of American Pit Bull Terriers and American Staffordshire Terriers is often enough to send chills down the backs of some fairly knowledgeable dog owners. This response does not address the fear that the name *pit bull* brings out in the average person. Pit-panic has spread virally around the United States and around the world. The result has fueled a negative media blitz, bogey-dog horror stories, and a ridiculous plethora of breed-specific bans and restrictions.

Contrast these negative perceptions with the real American Pit Bull Terrier (APBT) of the United Kennel Club (UKC) and the American Staffordshire Terrier (Amstaff) of the American Kennel Club (AKC). It is true that these breeds' ancestors were originally bred for fighting. It is true that the APBT/Amstaff is, pound for pound, one of the most powerful breeds of dog ever developed. It is true that they do have a very high pain threshold. The most ironic and astonishing truth of all is that there are thousands upon thousands of normal, well-adjusted, non-dog-fighting people and families who wouldn't own any dog other than an American Staffordshire Terrier or an American Pit Bull Terrier. These normal, average, everyday people will tell you that their APBT/Amstaff is a loyal, intelligent, clean, loving pet with an excellent temperament! These dogs have great potential. How they reach that potential is up to you.

# The Fighting Dog Heritage

The American Pit Bull Terrier and the Amstaff came about originally as an experiment in dog breeding between the solid, athletic bulldog types of over a century ago and fast, tough British terriers. This cross was to produce a pit fighting dog of speed, power, and exceptional grit or gameness (the ability to withstand pain without quitting). The dog breeders accomplished what they set out to do. Regardless of which expert you listen to, the bull-and-terrier fighting dogs have been around for well over 150 years.

The Great Dane was originally a boarhound. The Fox Terrier was originally bred to go into underground dens after foxes and run them out. The Bull Mastiff was originally a gamekeeper's dog used to bring down poachers. None of these breeds perform these original tasks today. About 99.9 percent of American Pit Bull Terriers and American Staffordshire Terriers do not do now what they were originally bred to do either. These dogs have been tarred with the brush of public mistrust that has been based on the actions of a "sport" that was outlawed nearly a century ago. The fact that a miniscule group of diehards continue it has had a horrendous impact on the breed.

# Their Recent Bad Reputation and How It Happened

Ironically, even with all the bad publicity, the American Pit Bull Terrier/Amstaff are very popular dogs. However, with popularity always comes a group of greedy, would-be dog breeders who want to cash in. Dogs that should never have been bred, even once, are bred repeatedly regardless of bad temperaments,

health problems, or genetic defects. Overbreeding of the poorest quality dogs will ultimately devastate any breed.

The American Pit Bull Terrier has become popular with some people for all the wrong reasons. The general public heard all the horror stories about this "canine monster" and some people just had to have one. The supply of poorly bred APBTs/Amstaffs caught up with the demand for the meanest, toughest dog on the block. The rest became a self-fulfilling prophecy. People who should have never owned a dog were able to get dogs that should never have been bred.

# Human Culprits

The American Pit Bull Terrier did not get a bad reputation all by itself. Quite a few humans have been guilty of a variety of misdeeds. Dog fighters have kept the image alive of the American Pit Bull Terrier as a savage killer. The breed-for-greed crowd that will mass-produce poor-quality APBTs/Amstaffs and then sell them to unsuspecting and unprepared members of the public deserves a lot of this guilt. The ignorant or uncaring dog buyer who purchases a dog just to have the meanest dog on the block owns a lot of responsibility along with a liberal dose of stupidity. The irresponsible APBT owner who doesn't have his or her dog spayed or neutered or trained and under control shares the blame. The members of the media who use the headline-grabbing words "pit bull" when they are not sure of the breed in order to sensationalize a dog bite or dog attack story should know better. The elected officials who have, through the threadbare blanket of reason for breed-specific legislation, targeted thousands upon thousands

of responsible owners and innocent canines just to target the miscreants should be ashamed of their profundity of overreaction. Those in the general public who have prejudicially passed judgment on several entire breeds and breed mixtures based on what was heard about a few dogs are as guilty as the rest!

## A Canine Loose Cannon?

Is the American Pit Bull Terrier a breed that is out of control? Are all APBTs/Amstaffs problems just waiting to happen? The answer to these questions is *no*. Some APBTs are out of control and dangerous, just as there are dogs of many other breeds that are out of control or danger-

ous. To say that the overwhelming majority of APBTs/Amstaffs are out of control is ludicrous and untrue.

The right APBT/Amstaff with a good temperament, if well socialized and given good training, will not be any more of a problem than any other breed and probably less of a problem than a number of breeds and mixtures of breeds! If the American Pit Bull Terrier or American Staffordshire Terrier were coming on the scene right now for the first time, perceptions would be vastly different! There would be no fighting dog history or stigma. The breed would not have been hurt by overbreeding of poor-quality dogs. Looking at the APBT/Amstaff with fresh eyes, as if for the first time, you would see two quite exceptional breeds of dog!

The Amstaff/APBT breed is of medium size. It has a short, easy-to-groom coat that comes in many attractive colors. The breed is large enough to be able to take the rough-housing that children bring, but small enough to fit right in with most families in their homes. Amstaffs and APBTs are usually easy to housetrain and do well in obedience training. They could be said to be protective, but no more protective than many other breeds. These breeds do not have a great many genetic problems, and are attractive, versatile dogs with many excellent qualities.

Is the APBT a canine loose cannon or an excellent all-around pet? That will depend largely on the dog's owner. If an owner takes time to find the right dog, carefully socializes him, thoroughly trains him, and provides for him in a responsible way, the odds are overwhelmingly in favor of the Amstaff/American Pit Bull Terrier being a superb pet. With the wrong owner, the American Staffordshire Terrier or APBT could be among the worst dogs to own. The irresponsible APBT/Amstaff owner could have a dog that could be as bad as any other breed of large or strong, potentially aggressive dogs in a similarly undisciplined situation! The type of owner is the key to the type of dog.

# SHOULD YOU OWN AN APBT/AMSTAFF TERRIER?

*Purchasing or adopting any breed of dog is a big responsibility, but the APBT/Amstaff has special needs. A prospective owner needs to become thoroughly familiar with the responsibilities that come with caring for one of these breeds.*

## Basic Dog Owner Responsibilities

Every owner of any breed or type of dog should be responsible, aware, and caring. Proper housing, medical care, food, training, and socialization are just some of the basic requirements that should be understood before anyone undertakes to own any dog.

Unless a potential dog owner is willing and able to give these essentials, dog ownership should be delayed or even avoided altogether. To own a pet and to not provide for his or her needs is certainly cruel, neglectful, and even illegal.

## Additional APBT/Amstaff Owner Responsibilities

Because of the controversy that surrounds the APBT, American Staffordshire Terrier, and similar dogs, potential owners of these dogs must be even more aware of their responsibilities than owners of many other breeds. The owner of an American Pit Bull Terrier or an Amstaff will need:

✔ A realistic, non-Pollyanna approach to a puppy or an older adopted dog that will need real care and attention.

✔ An aware, alert approach to APBT/Amstaff ownership, recognizing the need for a quality dog to be given quality care.

✔ An understanding that not everyone will welcome the presence of an Amstaff or an APBT in a neighborhood, a city park, or even on a public street accompanied by his owner!

✔ Adequate fencing, adequate housing, adequate training, positive attitudes about protecting an APBT or Amstaff from becoming lost, strayed, stolen, or involved in something that could bring harm.

✔ Previous personal experience with other kinds of dogs combined with a high degree of acquired knowledge about Amstaffs and APBTs.
✔ Serious consideration of not having an APBT or Amstaff be one's first dog.
✔ An understanding and protective attitude by all members of an APBT's or an Amstaff's household that the pet's control and safety should always be a prime consideration!

## A Male or a Female?

A female of any breed is generally a little less challenging for pet owners. Male dogs of most breeds tend to be more aggressive, not that females cannot be aggressive. Unneutered males will arduously pursue females in heat. In a neighborhood, this could lead to several kinds of negative consequences.

Discuss your personal preferences with several knowledgeable American Staffordshire Terrier or American Pit Bull Terrier breeders. Get them to assess your current situation as a potential dog owner. Weigh their advice along with what you believe is a wise course of action in gender selection. Combine this with the choice that makes the most common sense.

## A Puppy or an Older Dog?

There are going be some very excellent adult dogs available to you. If you have the experience and capacity to help an older Amstaff or APBT adjust to a new home and family, you perhaps could consider this option. But, as with a preference for males or females, adopting an adult in desperate need of a good home or buying a well-bred puppy is largely a personal decision.

An American Staffordshire or American Pit Bull Terrier puppy will have an opportunity to grow up as one of the family. When a family is well prepared for the addition of a puppy, the youngster can easily become an integral part of everyday activity.

An adopted American Staffordshire Terrier or American Pit Bull Terrier can also become a greatly beloved family pet. An adult adoptee

gives you the added knowledge that there are thousands of such dogs that are in foster care or animal shelters not for what they have done, but what has been done to them. Rehoming the right APBT or Amstaff can be among the most rewarding experiences in the entire pantheon of dog ownership!

## An APBT or an Amstaff?

Once upon a time in a dog universe not so far away, the American Pit Bull Terrier and the American Staffordshire Terrier were the same dog. Well over 100 years ago, the United Kennel Club was founded to register the pit dogs under the name American Pit Bull Terrier. In the 1930s the Ameri-

can Kennel Club renamed the breed as the Staffordshire Terrier (which became the American Staffordshire Terrier in the 1970s). Early on, there were dogs registered in both organizations and in the APBT-only organization, the American Dog Breeders Association (ADBA). In the past seven-plus decades the lines between the APBT and the American Staffordshire have become unblurred. They are now two separate breeds with a history of some common ancestors.

The Amstaff is now predominantly bred for its pet qualities, appearance, and for its dog show potential. As a rule, many American Stafford-shire Terriers are more standardized in appearance than the average APBT. Show qualities like broad heads and muscled bodies are more of an Amstaff trademark today. They are in the top 100 of the AKC's most popular breeds.

The American Pit Bull Terrier shows a greater diversity of appearance than does the Amstaff. This comes from the fact that there are a large number of breed-for-greed and backyard breeders producing a large number of lesser quality dogs that bear this breed name. The UKC also has some dedicated dog show breeders who are much more careful about how their APBTs are bred and who pay attention to breed details.

Decades ago, the great concern for American Staffordshire breeders was the amount of recent APBT heritage their dogs had. Today this has dramatically changed. According to the American Kennel Club, no American Pit Bull Terriers can be AKC-registered. The exact opposite is true with the United Kennel Club, as any AKC-registered Amstaff can be registered in the UKC as an American Pit Bull Terrier!

Whether to own an American Staffordshire Terrier or an American Pit Bull Terrier is purely a matter of personal choice. In the past, the *pit* part of the APBT name was enough to discourage some people from owning one. Some of these people turned to the American Staffordshire, which had been bred along AKC exhibition lines. You can find an Amstaff breeder (or an APBT breeder) near you by contacting the national clubs (see "Information," page 92).

# THE ADOPTION OPTION

*One of the perils of popularity is that thousands of otherwise healthy and good pet-quality dogs end up without a home. These American Pit Bull Terriers and American Staffordshire Terriers, through no fault of their own, end up in animal shelters where death is almost certain for many of them.*

## Effect and Cause

In every part of the United States, animal shelters are overflowing with wonderful pet prospects that have a very bleak future if someone does not come along and adopt them. A high proportion (as much as 40 percent in some shelters) of these dogs and puppies in need of homes are American Staffordshire Terriers, American Pit Bull Terriers, and mixes of these two and other similar breeds.

According to Pit Bull Rescue Central (PBRC), an excellent national clearinghouse for bull-breed dogs and mixes, thousands of homeless APBTs/Amstaffs and similar dogs are killed each year. This number, according to PBRC, amounts to 200 dogs and puppies each and every day just in the Los Angeles area alone. The reason for this horrendous statistic is that there are simply not enough homes for these potentially great pets.

One cause of this sad and despicable plight is the high popularity of Amstaffs and APBTs around the country. The breed-for-greed crowd could not care less if one of the puppies they sell (often for high prices) does not work out in his new home. This crowd does not care if the resulting youngster becomes homeless and ends up in a shelter where his future is practically nonexistent.

Also, part of the cause are the thugs, punks, and gangbangers who produce bad-tempered dogs for their nefarious activities. Often these dogs are turned out onto the streets where they become homeless and are subject to great danger.

Others implicated in the cause are the naïve backyard breeders who want to raise a litter or two for their own amusement. Often these puppies go to ill-prepared homes that are unable or unwilling to care for their new pets.

Many of these APBTs/Amstaffs go from poorly equipped homes to animal shelters.

## The Answer

You, the Amstaff or APBT potential owner, may be the ultimate solution to this epidemic. In the next chapter we deal with how to successfully purchase a puppy of one of these breeds. Perhaps you should skip that chapter and take your interest in these phenomenal dogs to a rescue organization (PBRC.com) or a local animal shelter and seek your next pet from among the homeless and helpless awaiting euthanasia.

Much of the rest of this book can be adapted to help you work with your new shelter-originated pet. Older dogs will need a little more patience and care to undo problems resulting from their previous homes or lack thereof. Having had many shelter dogs, I can assure you that the best pets are those you are saving by making them your own.

If a puppy from a breeder is what you really must have, remember something that your breeder must live with every time a litter is produced. For every puppy born at a breeder's, another one dies in a shelter! Countless American Pit Bull Terriers and Amstaffs (and similar dogs) await homes that may never come. Some of the greatest pets that have ever been born face the real likelihood that they will never live long enough to fulfill their destinies as pets.

## Concerns

Maybe you aren't sure what kind of dog you might get at a shelter or at one of the rescue organizations through Pit Bull Rescue Central. There are many excellent potential pet Amstaffs and APBTs in shelters throughout the country. Other dogs and puppies are in the hands of foster homes awaiting new, caring homes. In both settings, many of these dogs and puppies have been evaluated and found to be fine prospects for new owners.

APBTs and Amstaffs are quite resilient in their capacity to move on from a bad situation to a better one. Recently, a famous professional athlete was convicted of involvement in a dog-fighting ring. This sports star was sentenced to two years in prison and all of his dogs were seized. Long before the athlete was out of jail, several of his former fighting dogs had made the transition (with help from some caring people) from pit fighters to therapy dogs! These battle-scarred veterans are now going into

hospitals and nursing homes and providing the love and comfort that they themselves were denied for so long.

## Outcome

If you think the American Pit Bull Terrier or American Staffordshire Terrier is right for you, why not do the right thing and at least visit a nearby shelter? You can also see a long list of available dogs and puppies (many right where you are) arrayed on the website of Pit Bull Rescue Central. You may not find your dream dog, but then again, you might and you can not only gain a new best friend, but you can save a life as well.

# CONSIDERATIONS BEFORE BUYING/ADOPTING

*For you to have the best possible outcome with your Amstaff or American Pit Bull Terrier, you should start with the best possible puppy or a carefully evaluated older adoptable dog.*

## What You Should Expect

Most reputable Amstaff and APBT breeders will be as concerned about whether you should get one of their puppies as you are. This concern, often reflected in a number of questions from the breeder to you, is a good sign that this breeder really cares about finding loving, lifelong homes for all puppies produced.

**Price:** You should expect to pay a fair price, generally several hundred dollars, for a healthy pet prospect from stock with good temperaments. Healthy, well-dispositioned show prospects will cost you more depending on breeder and location. Beware of bargains; with Amstaffs and APBTs you positively cannot afford them. Bargain puppies often become much more expensive than many top show dogs would be!

**Ads:** Popularity has its perils. Especially for American Pit Bull Terriers, one can see many classified ads offering puppies in the Sunday newspapers in every major city. Some of these litters may possibly be from healthy dogs with excellent temperaments. More likely, these ads are reflective of a casual mating of two dogs that should have never been bred. You have a better chance finding buried treasure or striking oil in your backyard than in getting just the puppy you want in this manner.

**Shelters:** For adoptable Amstaffs or APBTs expect an animal shelter or rescue organization to give you the third degree about your aspirations as an APBT/Amstaff owner. You will need to show that you are capable of rehoming a dog or puppy in desperate need of a new life. You will also need to commit to the care and retooling of an animal that may have been abused or neglected. The caring people involved with pet adoptions want to make sure that a pet's new home is not just a repeat of his old home.

## Documents

There are several documents that you should receive:

**Health records:** This will be the puppy's medical history, showing the dates of all veterinarian examinations, wormings, vaccinations, and any treatments the puppy may have had and for what.

Adoptable pets will have recent records of what health care they have received in their shelter or foster home environments, but there may not be much about their early years. Any newly rehomed pet should have a complete physical and updated immunizations.

**The AKC or UKC registration papers:** These forms, from their respective kennel clubs, affirm that this Amstaff or American Pit Bull Terrier puppy is a purebred (his mother and father were purebreds and also registered). You should also get applications that you can send to the AKC or UKC (or both if the puppy's parents were both dual-registered) to register your puppy in your name.

Your shelter adult (or puppy) will probably not have registration papers or a pedigree. In one sense this may seem to be a real negative. In another sense you will be able to choose an adoptable Amstaff/APBT based on the magic that happens between you and the dog. Having adopted dogs, I know that this magic is a definite draw and is better in many ways than some documents attesting to the past of the animal.

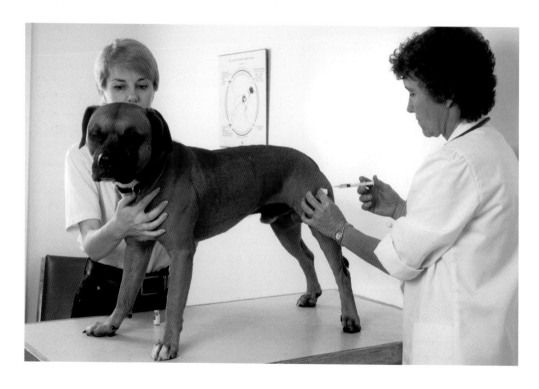

**Canine hip dysplasia (CHD) screening:** You will want test results pertaining to the parents of your puppy and their examinations for canine hip dysplasia (CHD) (see page 79). Although these results are not a guarantee that your puppy will be free from this ailment, CHD screening is the only predictive testing that may be currently available to you. OFA (Orthopedic Foundation for Animals) or CHD testing is performed for potential breeders when the stud dog or bitch is two years old.

**Note:** The Penn hip testing (which can be done only by specially trained veterinary practitioners) and some other forms of prescreening can be done on younger animals. You would be wise to use whatever testing is available to you to ascertain the hip health of your American Pit Bull Terrier or American Staffordshire Terrier.

**A rule concerning documents:** Before you become too attached to a puppy, make sure that the dog's papers are available to you. Quite simply, if they are not available, don't buy the puppy! Most reputable breeders are honest and are not out to cheat you. However, you want to avoid what could be called the "puppy buyer's lament," which is "The breeder said the papers are in the mail!"

# Guarantees

## Health/Temperament

All responsible Amstaff and American Pit Bull Terrier breeders will give you a reasonable and written health and temperament guarantee on any puppy you buy from them. This should state that the dog's inherited health and temperament are guaranteed. If an inherited problem occurs, you can return the puppy.

Confident breeders who have taken real care in choosing the ancestry of their dogs usually know from the breeding that a properly handled puppy will be healthy and have a good disposition.

## Spay/Neuter Agreement

You are not the only party in this agreement that will want a guarantee. Responsible dog breeders often ask for several written assurances from you regarding a puppy from their kennel. One of these involves the spaying or neutering of a pet quality dog or puppy. This is done to ensure that only the very best specimens are slated for the breeding pen. A spay/neuter agreement does not imply that your puppy is not a good, healthy animal. The only exception to the documents rule is that some breeders will hold registration papers until they receive proof that a veterinarian has spayed or neutered a pet puppy.

## Return Policy

Many reputable breeders have a return policy where they will want your puppy back if you find you cannot keep it. This strong proprietary interest in the future of a puppy is one of the best signs that you have chosen a quality breeder. Responsible breeders don't want their puppies to end up chained to the bumper of a wrecked car in a junkyard, given to the mysterious "friend in the country," or sent to almost certain death at an animal shelter.

If you are adopting a new pet, the animal shelter or rescue organization will want to be certain that if you and your Amstaff/APBT do not, for some reason, work out, that the pet will be returned to the shelter or organization. Every effort is made to match up dogs in need of homes with homes in need of dogs. Your

commitment is important, but so is the quality of the new life for the adoptee.

# Selecting the Right Puppy

Suppose you have decided you want a female American Staffordshire Terrier with some obedience trial potential. Because you have taken time to concentrate on the traits you would like to have in your new pet, you have a better chance of avoiding first-puppy-syndrome. All Amstaff puppies tend to be adorable and an impulsive person or family can undo all the long hours of study and research by falling in love with the first puppy or with the first litter seen. That first puppy may indeed be the best for you, but it will still be the best after you have looked at as many puppies as possible.

## Socialization

A good breeder will have already begun the crucial socialization process with this litter.

The puppies should be at ease and even curious and happy to see strangers. Their mother should be alert but not threatened by your presence, and if you can see the puppies' sire (father), approach, and pet him, you may be about to buy a puppy.

# Selecting the Right Shelter/Rescue Animal

As with choosing a puppy from a breeder, have in mind what gender and other variables you would like to have in your adopted pet. Be prepared however to have your preconceived notions dashed when you connect with that one perfect homeless APBT.

Look at several prospects. Discuss what information is available about each one of them. Count on the shelter staff or rescue members to tell you as much as they know and what they have learned about potential pets for you and your family.

Gender, color, and specific age requirements may go out the window when you see more American Staffordshires and American Pit Bull Terriers than you can ever hope to adopt. Temper that realization with the knowledge that for many of these shelter and rescue animals, you may be their last chance. Ponder over the animals that best seem to fit your lifestyle and wishes, but remain flexible about your final choice.

The shelter or rescue people will tell you the pluses and minuses about each possibility. It is up to you to visualize how your desire and ability to provide a good home will mesh with each dog or puppy. Many of the same responsibilities that involve a purchased puppy or adult are in play with an adopted pet. Shelter and adoptee animals desire just the same care and

environment that a show specimen from a pricey breeder would merit.

An additional point that many people who have adopted dogs are enthusiastic about sharing involves the happiness of a rescued pet. Many accounts point to the seeming extra love that such dogs want to share with their families, after they have finally found those families!

# Before You Bring Your APBT/Amstaff Home

Well before the time that you enter your home with your new Amstaff or American Pit Bull Terrier puppy or adopted pet you must do many things to get ready.

Because your pet will need to live in the house with you, you will need to make the home safe for the inquisitive, chewing youngster or for a new adult dog.

✔ You will need to work out your plan to housetrain the puppy and possibly the adult.

✔ You will need to make some necessary purchases.

✔ You will want to assess each area to which the puppy will have access for things that might harm him.

## Essential Purchases

**Food:** The first essential purchase and one of the most important is to buy some of the exact same food the breeder has been feeding your new puppy, unless the breeder has been having trouble with this particular food. You can change diets, if you absolutely must, at some later date. Do not change a new puppy's food—doing so can only add to the trauma the youngster is already experiencing! Feeding an adult is no less important and a quality food is absolutely required.

**Cage/crate:** Because your Amstaff or APBT should live indoors with you, the next purchase of greatest importance is a dog cage/crate/carrier, which will serve as your pet's home within your home. (See Crate Training, page 58).

**Water and food bowls:** Your new family member will need his own water and food bowls. Remember the powerful jaws of these dogs and get dishes made of strong metal or ceramic material. Get a sturdy, flat-bottomed design that is large enough for permanent use and that will not be easily tipped over.

**Collar and leash:** Use your pet products store professional's experience to get a leash (also called a lead) with an appropriately sized collar for your new pet. This leather, nylon, or web material collar will be the dog's regular collar. Because training begins early with American Pit Bull Terriers and American Staffordshires, you will also need a training collar for either a puppy or a dog.

**Brush:** Ask your pet product's store professional about the right brush for the puppy's short, smooth coat. A smooth-bristle brush or a rubber-cleated glove ("Love Glove" is one model) is a good way to introduce your dog to the needed and enjoyable role of regular brushing. Like most things with Amstaffs and APBTs, the earlier you start something, the easier it will be. Even though these dogs shed very little and require little grooming, you will want to get the puppy accustomed to the brush while he is still very young, for those times when brushing is needed. An adult dog will also appreciate being gently brushed and groomed.

**Toothbrush:** Another essential early purchase is your puppy's own toothbrush. By initiating teeth cleaning while the puppy is still small, it won't be a problem when the dog is older (and stronger). A toothbrush for your adopted adult is also a good investment.

**Toys:** Toys for the American Staffordshire Terrier and the American Pit Bull Terrier differ from those for many other breeds. The strength of these dogs, even as puppies, can reduce even tough-looking chew toys into rubble in a surprisingly short time. Try hard rubber and strong nylon chewing items ("Kong" and "Nylabone" are two brand names). These dogs have a great potential for intestinal blockage because they swallow pieces of what seemed to be indestructible toys. Ask your pet products' professional for recommendations about the best chew items for your Amstaff/APBT.

## The Cage/Crate/Carrier

Certainly the best reason for sharing your home with your new pet is that he desperately needs your companionship and supervision. Human interaction or the lack thereof is responsible for some of the misbehavior that can be legitimately pinned on purebred APBTs or Amstaffs.

Your Amstaff/APBT (puppy or adult) is, like the wolf and coyote, a denning animal. In the wild, canines will have a den of some sort most of their lives. This instinctive behavior is just as true of the American Staffordshire Terrier and the American Pit Bull Terrier. Even if your pet lives inside with you he needs a place of his own.

Various models are available on the market. They range from the fiberglass airline-type carriers to cages to crates. An airline crate is most often recommended because of the sturdy construction and versatile style. Crates and cages are also quality suggestions.

The cage or crate is not only a humane way to keep your pet where you want him to be, it also makes use of the denning instinct. The crate-training concept is also a wonderful aid in housetraining (see HOW-TO: Housetraining, page 70) and in giving your new pet his own place to sleep.

## The Fenced Yard

If you and your family are fortunate enough to live where you can have a fenced backyard, this will be a real benefit for your APBT/Amstaff. You will be able to give the dog a longer outside break than you may be able to on walks. If you have the option, make your fence strong, high, and tunnel-resistant. If you cannot do this, don't leave your dog unattended in the backyard!

Making your home and area safe for your new APBT or Amstaff puppy is a little different than it would be for a puppy of most other breeds. You will want to decide just where the puppy will be allowed to go. Not every part of any home is a good place for a curiosity-filled little terrier. Stairwells, balconies, and other potentially dangerous locations should be off-limits. Here are some ways to accomplish this very important task:

✔ Get down to the puppy's level and look for things or situations where a little dog could get hurt. This is a great, fun, and instructive chore in which children could help!

✔ Look for electrical cords, low-sitting houseplants, doorstops, and other everyday items that might cause harm to a chewing puppy.

✔ Reposition any heavy items that the puppy could pull over onto himself.

✔ Make a diligent search (perhaps with the children again) for foreign objects that a puppy could swallow. These could include thumbtacks, pins, pencils, coins, beads, batteries, and so forth. This search is especially important in carpeted areas.

✔ Check your home for any exposed woodwork, especially in older homes, that could have lead-based paint that could poison a gnawing puppy.

✔ Be certain that your puppy isn't exposed to areas, furniture, or carpeting that have been treated with chemicals, pesticides, or possibly toxic sprays. This certainly includes any areas where poisons may have been placed (and possibly forgotten) for rats, mice, roaches, or ants.

✔ Close off any spaces behind televisions, upright pianos, couches, or other heavy furniture in which a youngster could get trapped. This includes railings or banisters where a puppy's head might get stuck.

✔ Puppy-proofing also includes thoroughly training the entire family about what should and should not be done when the puppy is around. Care should be taken to prevent a puppy from rushing out a door and into harm's way. Family members should open doors carefully to avoid crushing a little terrier behind them. No cars should move in a garage or

*Puppy proofing includes protecting a teething puppy from chewing electric cords.*

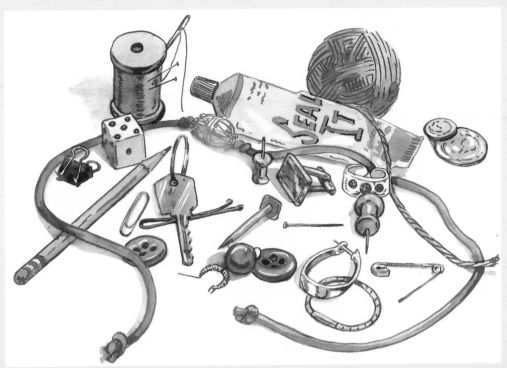

*Pick up any and all items that a curious puppy could swallow.*

driveway until the driver is *absolutely* certain the puppy is not under the vehicle. Family members should be careful to avoid stepping on the puppy.

✔ Make appropriate use of your puppy's crate (see The Cage/Crate/Carrier, page 34).

✔ Most puppy-proofing involves common sense. However, by taking an organized approach, you will be less likely to miss something that could injure your new family member. Protecting a new puppy shouldn't be an afterthought; it should be an always thought.

# BRINGING YOUR APBT/AMSTAFF TERRIER HOME

*The first few weeks and months in the life of your American Pit Bull Terrier or American Staffordshire Terrier puppy will most likely set the tone for what kind of dog he will become. The first important steps toward socializing and training your new dog should have been started before you ever saw him.*

## First Things First

Initial training is done by a dog's mother. The breeder should have started early socialization. Unless these two things have occurred, the psychological makeup of the resulting puppy may well be incomplete throughout his entire life.

The need for this early socialization underscores the importance of picking the right breeder from whom to obtain a puppy. Responsible breeders know that some human interaction must begin even before the puppy's eyes are open and must continue in a consistent manner throughout much of the youngster's first year.

**Note:** Most of the suggestions made here for puppies are equally applicable for adopted adults. In most situations with an adult pet brought into a new home, the lessons are similar. Be especially aware that your new adopted pet may have learned some bad habits in his previous life. You and the dog will have to work through these lessons together and you can if you will try.

## Socialization

Socializing a puppy literally means introducing him to new things and people in a nonthreatening manner. This socialization process

## TIP

### Get off to a Good Start

Try, if at all possible, to have a responsible adult home with the puppy for the first several days to a week. Taking several days off from work to help this young, invited guest get off to a great start in your home is time well spent and can shorten this all-important adjustment time in the life of the puppy.

Amstaff or American Pit Bull Terrier puppies are like little learning sponges soaking up information from their earliest sentient moments. Because dogs use their sense of smell even more than their sense of hearing and their hearing more than their sense of sight, the first human scents that come their way will be registered while the pups are still blind newborns. What they hear, in terms of tones rather than actual words, will become part of their inventory of threatening or nonthreatening stimuli.

The right kind of socialization will introduce the puppies to different types of people: males, females, children, older people, and people from ethnic groups other than that of the breeder. In this way, the mental and acceptance horizons of a very young puppy are broadened to include many different humans. The puppy learns that humans, as a group, pose no threat. Some breeds become thoroughly socialized more easily than others. However, most experts agree that the canine that becomes the best companion or pet is the one that receives the best socialization.

makes the difference in whether an animal will be wild or tame, and comfortable around humans or afraid of them. All the stories about dogs being born in the wild or wild wolves becoming like lap dogs after meeting the right human are just stories.

Animals begin to learn early as a part of basic survival. It is generally true that a dog that has not bonded with humans before he is 12 weeks old is not ever likely to do so. When the dog in question is one of the most powerful canine athletes on earth, the matter of socialization takes on even greater significance.

## Timeline

The timeline for socialization is crucial. Most breeders believe that bonding with humans must begin and, to a large extent, be accomplished within the first six weeks of a puppy's life. Authorities differ on the exact age. However, most believe that without appropriate, gentle, thorough socialization, a dog will never reach his potential as a pet or companion.

Socialization for a new adult is somewhat different. With an APBT/Amstaff you have to be sure that your pet is not overly aggressive. You may know this information from the animal shelter or the rescue organization. Even so, carefully (and with a stout leash and collar) make introductions to other people and dogs. You may find that your dog will surprise you by his good temperament. Still, always be in control!

# Adjustment Time

It is important to remember that the puppy can certainly be stressed by being abruptly uprooted from the only world he has ever known. Be gentle with the new puppy. This will help him get the best possible start in his new home. Even the trip home in a car can be stressful; this is one time that a dog may not need to be in a carrier. Have an adult member of the family securely and safely hold the puppy during the ride. (It may be advisable to have this person wear old clothes and bring some old towels in case of motion sickness or other mishaps.)

Training for your new puppy begins immediately. Some dog experts advise that you should already have an outdoor area picked out as a urine and feces relief site. You may be able to

*pre-scent* this location with some droppings or litter from the puppy's first home. Immediately upon arriving home, take the puppy to this site and wait until the puppy relieves himself. The smell of urine or droppings should encourage the puppy to perform. When it does, as it generally will, enthusiastically praise the puppy. This first natural activity will be the puppy's first success and will begin his training process with you.

Your puppy should arrive at your home when he can be the center of attention and will not be neglected or ignored in any way. This pretty well eliminates Christmas puppies as a good idea unless the puppy is the only gift anyone gets that season. The puppy has no idea where he is and has only vague realizations of who you and your family are. He will need a lot of love and consistent care to help lessen the trauma of this time.

Your APBT or Amstaff puppy will not just automatically know the things you will want him to know any more than a human infant would be able to function without someone to guide and teach it. No one in the puppy's new home should be harsh or severe toward the puppy during this time. The puppy needs to learn his first lessons in his new home in a warm, trusting, and supportive environment.

Be equally diligent in introducing your new adult dog into your home. Help him settle in and come to bond with and trust you and your family. As with a puppy, a supportive environment will work wonders with most dogs.

# The Cage/Crate/Carrier

Your American Staffordshire Terrier or American Pit Bull Terrier will always be a better pet and companion if he remains in close contact with you. As you allow your puppy to live with you, you will discover key things about this little canine that you will probably miss or that won't even manifest themselves if the puppy is sadly relegated to a kennel or backyard existence. The puppy will also learn things from you by being in close proximity that he will never learn if he becomes the dog out back.

The greatest aid to allowing your dog to live comfortably under the same roof with you and your family is the cage, crate, or carrier. Most often recommended are the fiberglass airline-type crates that have great strength and versatility. Utilizing the natural instinct the dog has to be a denning creature will not only be a better way to share living quarters, but it is also better for the dog.

Your purchase of such a den substitute should occur before you bring your Amstaff or APBT puppy home for the first time. After you have given the puppy a chance to be a star by performing correctly at the preset waste relief site, you can bring the youngster inside. After a few minutes of welcoming the puppy home, you can introduce what will become his own place within your household—the cage/crate/carrier. Bring a toy or perhaps an old blanket from the puppy's original home—the litter box—to infuse his new home with familiar scents and smells. Everyone in your family must understand that this crate is not a tiny prison. They should know that the puppy will need a place of his own and that his successful integration into the family will go much more smoothly with a crate than without. There is no cruelty or harshness in helping a puppy by letting him have his own crate. In addition, the process of housetraining is greatly enhanced by working with the natural processes relating to den behavior.

## Location

Place the crate somewhere that is out of the way but not isolated. Choose a location out of direct sunlight and out of drafts. Pick a spot that will let the puppy see what is going on in the room when he is in the crate, but that doesn't sit right in the main walking area.

Your puppy will want to be a part of things, but the den is supposed to be a place to go to rest or just take time out.

## Getting Acquainted

When you first introduce your new APBT or Amstaff to your home, let him have a chance to get acquainted with his new family in his new surroundings. No roughhousing activity with the youngster now; play only gently. Watch the puppy to see if he needs to make a trip back to the relief area. If he does show any sign of wanting to urinate or defecate, quickly and gently pick him up and head to the relief spot. If you make it in time and the puppy uses the area, always praise him lavishly. This is the next step in housetraining your puppy.

## Play

Keep playtimes brief with the puppy in the initial days. As he begins to tire, gently move him to the home-scented crate or carrier. You want the puppy to associate being tired with going to this place of rest. Simply place the little one in the crate or carrier, shut the door, and walk away.

There are two aspects of the APBT or the Amstaff that work against each other here. These breeds generally have a lot of endurance, even as puppies. They also are generally very bright. The humans in your household have to show restraint in keeping playtimes brief and not depend on the puppy for a sign that he is tired. Also, the puppy will learn from your consistent repetition that the crate is the place to go for a rest. Smart terrier puppies will sometimes go to the crate all by themselves for a little nap or just a short break. Associating the den with sleep is a very important lesson for your puppy to learn.

Your American Staffordshire or American Pit Bull Terrier puppy will now have to adjust to life without his mother and littermates. This adjustment is one the puppy and your family must learn together!

## Learning About His Crate

The lesson for you and your family is that the puppy must be allowed to learn *his* lesson—the crate is for rest and sleeping, especially at night! The most important rule on this subject is that *nobody* gives in to feeling sorry for the lonely, whining, or crying puppy. If you or someone in your family responds to each whimper and cry that the lonely youngster makes, the lesson will not be lost on the puppy. "If I want them to come to hold or play with me, all I have to do is cry." This is not the lesson you want your puppy to learn!

A sad, lonely, crying canine baby is not a happy vision. An even sadder vision is the sad, lonely, crying canine adult that has become neurotic about being left alone at night. Being left in his crate at night will not harm your puppy. Thousands of potentially good house pets have been allowed to become hopeless and neurotic housepets because someone weakened at the first sound of sadness.

## Helping Your Puppy Settle In

You can help your APBT or Amstaff settle in with less trauma in many ways. You may have already started by providing a toy or blanket

with familiar smells on it. You can speak to a lonely, crated puppy sparingly, but with a calm and reassuring tone. This will let him know that you aren't far away.

## Food

Another key area of the settling-in process involves what the puppy eats. Unless otherwise recommended by the breeder, you should have obtained some of the same food he was eating at his first home. Shifting foods now can be a serious mistake and should not be undertaken without legitimate reasons. Dietary changes may bring on bowel upsets and even an increase in stress level for the puppy. Diarrhea may come about because of the trauma of the move. Your puppy should always have a good, consistent diet, probably of a premium dry food.

# The Crucial Early Lessons

You have brought your Amstaff or APBT puppy home. He has had a successful first experience (with much accompanying praise) at the relief site. Your family and you have made the youngster feel welcome and happy to be in his new home. Each of you was firm in not giving in when the puppy cried the first few nights in his crate. You gave him the same brand of quality puppy food that he had been eating and his system quickly got over move-related diarrhea. The puppy, in spite of a few little mistakes, is almost completely housetrained.

You now have helped the settling-in process take place. Much of what the puppy learns from now on will be additional lessons in good behavior. Consistency is vital here as in every area of pet ownership. These dogs, the Ameri-

can Pit Bull Terrier and the American Stafford-shire Terrier, are quite intelligent and remember much more than you think they will. If a 15-pound (6.8-kg) puppy is allowed on the couch, the same dog as a 60-pound (27.2-kg) adult will expect to be allowed on the couch. If Bruiser is not allowed as an adult to do what he did as a puppy, he will stubbornly remember this as something inconsistent.

Many of the puppy-targeted subjects and ideas work equally with older dogs. Always remember that your new pet needs a great amount of love and patience when he first moves into your home. While some puppy top-ics may seem unnecessary for an adult, the rationale behind them fits both insecure new puppies and insecure new grown dogs. Dogs, like most children, are great at testing the lim-its. They will want to see how far they can go this time with an activity that was not clearly stopped last time. A thoughtful and caring American Pit Bull Terrier or Amstaff owner won't subject a dog to these Jekyll and Hyde actions. Simply put, a puppy must be gently, but firmly, taught the behaviors that you will expect of him as an adult. A lot of potentially great dogs of many breeds have been almost ruined by inconsistent behavior from their owners. Don't do this to your APBT or American Staffordshire!

# UNDERSTANDING YOUR APBT/AMSTAFF TERRIER

*Like other breeds, the American Pit Bull Terrier and the American Staffordshire Terrier will become what their breeding, socialization, training, and care (or lack thereof) allow them to become. For their size, height, and weight, there are no more powerful dogs in the world. Their fighting legacy, their overall musculature, can be developed in either a positive way or a negative way.*

The APBT or the Amstaff can be among the best of pets for an aware and responsible dog owner. In the hands of a malevolent, neglectful, or ignorant owner, the same dog could become a canine menace. The breeding, socialization, training, and, most of all, the owner of an APBT or an Amstaff, will determine which of these dogs will emerge!

## The APBT/Amstaff as a Canine Companion

The American Staffordshire Terrier and the American Pit Bull Terrier can be excellent companion dogs for the caring and consistent owner. Dedication to their humans is a breed trait, but sometimes protectiveness is too.

The wise owner will do everything possible to foster, develop, encourage, and ensure the dog's positive traits.

Well-bred, well-trained APBTs or Amstaffs are excellent family dogs. Thousands of people enjoy them as pets without any problems. These dogs are family-oriented pets that represent no threat to anyone! The problems attributed to *pit bulls* have generally been seen in poorly bred and non-trained animals that had not been adequately socialized to other animals or to people. A powerful, active dog (of any breed or mixture of breeds) needs to have an excellent temperament and be thoroughly trained. Without these essentials, trouble awaits.

The APBT or the Amstaff is certainly not the right pet for everyone. A powerful dog will

Staffordshire Terrier is someone who has a good understanding of dogs from personal experience. This person is usually willing to seek out just the right dog. This potential dog owner will want to assume the socializing and training responsibilities that will help develop the dog of his or her choice into an excellent canine citizen. This potential owner will provide good care for the APBT or Amstaff and will ensure that the dog has the right food, lodging, veterinary care, and human interaction.

## The APBT/Amstaff and Children

The well-bred, well-socialized, well-trained American Pit Bull Terrier is usually less of a threat to children than the children are to him! An overwhelming majority of dog bites in the United States involve dogs other than the APBT. Many of these bites come from toy breeds and inbred or poorly bred dogs of faddish popularity. The number of bites relates directly to immense popularity and casual breeding backgrounds of many of these dogs.

Most responsible breeders of Amstaffs and APBTs raise their dogs with their children. These knowledgeable dog people train their dogs *and* their children to understand and appropriately interact with one another. Certainly some Amstaffs and APBTs have bitten humans, some of whom were children, but so have dogs of every breed! Some breeds are overwhelmingly greater potential biters than the APBT/Amstaff.

### Teaching Your Children Dog Safety

Children need to be taught how to approach strange dogs of any breed, just as dogs need to

need adequate control and some older people and children cannot physically supply that control. A first-time dog owner, in the minds of many experienced dog breeders, should probably not buy an APBT or Amstaff! An insecure person who wants only an aggressive dog to bolster some personal human inadequacy should never own one of these dogs. An uncaring or negligent person should not get an Amstaff or an APBT (or any other dog for that matter)!

The best candidate for ownership of an American Pit Bull Terrier or an American

# CHECKLIST

## Signs for Safety

Children need to learn a dog's body language that says approaching may not be safe and to never approach a dog showing the following signs:

**1.** Aggression—ruffled hair on his back and neck (the dog tries to be as large as he can be), stiffness, ears and tail erect and not at ease, possible growling, and a generally challenging posture.

**2.** Frightened—cringing, ground-hugging, trying to be as small as possible, tail down on the ground or held tightly between his legs, and a generally terrified or suspicious posture.

**3.** Injured—possibly lying down, whimpering, and even loudly crying with pain.

**4.** A dog that is eating and that wants to protect his food.

**5.** A male dog intent on pursuing or even mating with a female.

**6.** A mother dog with puppies.

be socialized to and with children. Children need to learn correct behavior around dogs. They must learn not to attempt to take away a dog's food, not to approach an injured animal, and not to act in a way (for example staring into the dog's face) that could be perceived by the dog as threatening. Dogs need good training and need to be in a household where all humans, including children, have a higher ranking in the pack (see Pack Behavior and Your APBT/Amstaff, page 56) than the dogs. Try to remember the following tips when introducing children to any dog:

✔ Children need to speak calmly to a dog and slowly offer a hand for the animal to sniff as an introduction.

✔ Children should be taught not to run away from a dog as this may encourage a chase.

✔ Children should avoid loud or rough playing around a protective dog.

# The APBT/Amstaff and Other Dogs

Dogs that are strangers will test the limits of each other, not unlike some school boys on the playground. When an APBT or an Amstaff, with

=== TIP ===

### Altercations with Another Dog

Take no chances in allowing your American Pit Bull Terrier or American Staffordshire Terrier to become involved in an altercation with another dog. The way public sentiment runs in many places, even if your dog is innocent of provocation, he will be blamed and you possibly prosecuted!

his ancestral pit-dog background, is confronted by another dog, a conflict is always possible. This is true of all breeds. That an APBT or an Amstaff is involved should only increase the human control factors that should always be present.

Because no dog, not just an Amstaff or an APBT, should be allowed to run around freely in a neighborhood, contacts between strange dogs should always be under controlled circumstances. During walks on the street or in the park, the APBT or Amstaff should be controlled by the following:

**1.** A knowledgeable, aware owner who is physically and mentally capable of avoiding obvious troublesome situations;

**2.** Thorough training that should make the Amstaff or APBT obedient to every command, even when under considerable stress;

**3.** A sturdy collar and lead (leash) that an alert owner holds securely.

## The APBT/Amstaff and Other Pets

A home with other pets needs to take the same wise precautions with Amstaffs and APBTs that it would with any other breed. Until an adult dog of any breed understands that other pets belong in the home and are not to be chased or harmed, he must be constantly monitored by humans when in the presence of these other pets.

A puppy being brought into a home with other animals can be socialized to accept these other pets as part of the living arrangements. An adequately socialized APBT or Amstaff is no more a threat to other pets than any other dog with similar socialization and training.

## The APBT/Amstaff and Guests in the Home

Many guests find that the only threat they face from most American Pit Bull Terriers or Amstaffs is being licked to death. These are, by nature, friendly dogs that will shower a friend of the master or mistress with considerable affection.

Normally a guest in the home will be accepted after being welcomed by a dog's owner. Threatening actions may attract a dog's attention; however, a friendly guest should have no cause for apprehension.

Dogs do seem to sense fear in a person and some people have developed what amounts to a phobia about dogs in general and the pit bull specifically. If a guest has such feelings, legitimate or otherwise, perhaps a prudent dog owner should be gracious and put the dog in his kennel, crate, or some other place away from the guest.

## The APBT/Amstaff and Strangers

As with guests in the home, a stranger may find APBTs or Amstaffs mainly friendly and curious. Another irony is that these breeds do not make exceptional guard dogs. Although their presence and their reputations make them a considerable deterrent to trespassers, most well-bred, well trained, well socialized APBT/Amstaffs will pose no danger to a mannerly stranger.

The wise dog owner keeps pets under control, thus avoiding accidental confrontations that could lead to trouble. By having a fenced yard or by keeping the APBT/Amstaff inside or in a kennel area, most negative or incidental interaction with strangers can be prevented.

## The APBT/Amstaff in the Neighborhood

Horror stories about pit bulls abound and may impact on a pet owner's relationship with the neighborhood. That *no* APBT or Amstaff should be allowed to run loose should go without saying. Letting an APBT/Amstaff run loose shows a lack of regard for one's neighbors and is probably against the law. Using fences, kennels, and leashes makes for good neighbors!

Some communities, states, counties, and even countries have enacted banning legislation against certain breeds of dogs, among them the APBT/Amstaff. These laws are probably nonsensical in most cases because they are often unenforceable and misdirected. However, they are in place and should be taken into consideration before purchasing a dog that would fall under such legal restrictions.

# CARING FOR YOUR APBT/AMSTAFF TERRIER

*When you bring a puppy or adult APBT/Amstaff into your home, you must assume total responsibility for the care of this pet. Without your care, the dog is doomed to fail to reach his potential and you are doomed to have a lesser pet than you wanted.*

## Keeping Your APBT/Amstaff Out of Bad Spots

A dog is still a dog, even with all his good points. Dogs, like children, may not always recognize potential danger or situations. The humans in the dog's family must keep the animal out of harm's way.

✔ Begin leash training very early with your APBT/Amstaff. These dogs can be very strong pullers. One 60-pound (27.2-kg) dog, in a contest, pulled a load weighing over a ton. Children and smaller adults cannot hope to stop an energetic and enthusiastic APBT or Amstaff by body weight or brute force!

✔ Do not ever let your pet run free in the neighborhood, in the park, at the beach, or anywhere it might encounter another dog or a similar dangerous situation.

✔ By starting at the earliest age, make it absolutely clear that you will not allow aggressive behavior toward another animal or human.

✔ Make certain that your backyard or kennel fence is strong enough and tall enough to keep an unsupervised pet contained. (Better yet, do not leave an unsupervised APBT/Amstaff outside!)

✔ When out on walks with your APBT/Amstaff and encountering other dogs (with their owners or without them), be smart and don't let even a minor confrontation with your dog get started. APBTs and Amstaffs are pretty smart and may remember that one time you seemed to encourage aggressive behavior. Consistency is your best training aid!

✔ Remember that just the presence of your dog may frighten some people. Don't let someone else's fear or overreaction cause your pet to become threatened.

# Exercise

Your pet should get regular daily exercise. This could come in the form of walks with you, romps with the children in the backyard, or in controlled runs (on leash). You don't have to run a marathon with your APBT/Amstaff because a pet in good condition who is being correctly fed will get by on moderate physical exercise.

Your dog's strong jaws will need a durable, nonsplintering chew toy, perhaps made of hardened rubber or nylon (see Essential Purchases, page 25), to allow him to work off some energy chewing each day.

# Grooming

As with so many other aspects of APBT/Amstaff ownership, grooming should begin in early puppyhood both as a cosmetic activity and as a part of the youngster's training. Brushing, bathing, teeth cleaning, and nail trimming are all much easier to accomplish on a powerful adult dog that had these things introduced to him when he was very young.

Grooming your Amstaff or American Pit Bull Terrier puppy should be done in a serious way. Choose a place and time that will be free of distractions. Handle the grooming as an adjunct to the training process. The puppy must be made to understand that this is not playtime, but it can be a pleasant time with you.

**Brushing:** Brushing not only helps to keep the skin invigorated by removing dead hair and skin, dirt, and any foreign matter that may have gotten on the dog, but it actually eliminates the need for a lot of baths.

**Bathing:** Bathing your dog too often will actually do harm to his skin and coat. The skin and hair can become dried out and the natural luster and shine of the coat diminished.

**Eyes and Ears:** Pay particular attention to the areas around the eyes and ears. These areas can be cleaned with a damp washcloth.

Regular brushing and grooming not only makes a pleasurable experience for the puppy, but it will give you a good opportunity to discover the presence of any skin problems, minor wounds, or parasites (mites, ticks, and fleas). Your consistent attention to your pet's cleanliness needs will be amply repaid with a more presentable pet and with the additional opportunity for bonding with the animal that a few moments of brushing can bring.

**Incidentals:** Make sure your puppy's collar, lead, and toys are occasionally cleaned to stop the spread of germs. Wiping them down with a disinfectant will also keep them looking bright and neat. Apply this same approach to the crate, the kennel area, and doggy door (if you have one).

# Feeding

Your American Pit Bull Terrier or American Staffordshire Terrier will need the best quality food available to keep in good shape and good energetic form. As with high-quality puppy food, casually (and negligently) changing diets for adult dogs is unwise. Find a premium dry dog food and stick to it. Change only when your veterinarian advises it. Quality canned foods and semimoist products can be used occasionally to spice up a dry ration, but remember that canned and semimoist forms can lead more quickly to obesity and should be used accordingly.

# Housetraining

When you first bring your APBT/Amstaff home, you will soon find that housetraining is a significant responsibility. It's important to spend the time to housetrain your APBT/Amstaff and take the necessary steps to make this an easy and rewarding experience for both you and your beloved pet.

Crate training works best and is the preferred method because your puppy instinctively will not want to eliminate in the area where he sleeps. However, there are other methods, such as paper training, if crate training is not practical for your lifestyle. (For more on housetraining, see HOW-TO: Housetraining, page 70.)

## Paper Training

A less effective and certainly less efficient way to housetrain a puppy involves the use of newspapers placed all over the floor in some easy-to-clean room such as a spare bathroom or a laundry room. Rather than someone being available to help the youngster make it outside to the relief spot, the puppy is placed in this papered room and left there.

Crate training makes housetraining so much easier that it almost makes paper training an unnecessary discussion; however, it may be helpful for some people. Some lifestyles make taking a puppy from his crate and hustling him outside to the relief site difficult. Apartment dwellers, for example, may find that taking a puppy down several flights to a pre-set location rapidly is a difficult task.

Other people find they must leave the puppy alone for several hours or even all day. You could not leave a very young puppy in his crate under such conditions. Paper training is a

Older Amstaffs and APBTs need less in the way of fats and more in the way of carbohydrates. Senior formulations of the same brand you have been using will generally work well for older dogs. They also may be recommended by your veterinarian for spayed or neutered dogs. Since most adult dogs should be spayed or neutered, paying attention to their diet is crucial.

On the rare occasion that you have to completely change a diet, do so very gradually for a month-long trial. Slowly introduce increasingly greater percentages of a new diet into a mixture with the existing food. Table scraps, leftovers, and so-called home cooking are generally a bad choice of nourishment for dogs. Avoid unnecessary food changes that can really mess up a dog's dietary balance.

substitute, but not really an equal substitute to crate training. It will be slower and less attuned to the way the adult dog will need to function. However, if used consistently, it does provide an alternative of sorts.

Paper training involves confining the puppy in the papered room. It does not work particularly well with the crate training/timed outside visit method, because the puppy will suddenly be given two right places to defecate and urinate rather than the one special site (see Crate Training, page 70). Paper training will require three distinct areas in the confinement room:

**1.** a waste elimination area,

**2.** a food and water area, and

**3.** a sleeping or rest area where the puppy's crate is located.

✔ The floor of the waste area should be covered with several layers of spread-out newspapers. Using layers will allow the top sheets to be soiled or wet and then removed. The puppy's scent will remain behind on the lower layers and will thus reinforce this as the relief place.

✔ Because puppies naturally will not want to urinate or defecate near their food, water, and sleeping areas, these areas should be as far away from the designated waste area as possible.

✔ Paper training can be combined with outside visits early in the morning and late at night. Always be lavish with praise if the puppy defecates or urinates outside.

✔ A further way to combine the lesser effective paper method with the more effective use of an outside area is to make the waste area in the confinement room smaller and smaller as your puppy matures. Gradually, a puppy or young dog can be transferred completely outside. This will then require a complete deodorizing (and scent neutralizing) of the room and a shift to the crate training/timed outside visit method.

# TRAINING YOUR APBT/AMSTAFF TERRIER

*Any dog of any size will need appropriate training. Failure to provide this training will usually result in a poor companion animal. A poor companion animal is a danger to himself or to other creatures—human and animal. Training for the APBT and Amstaff is an important enough consideration to make it an absolute. Don't own an untrained American Staffordshire Terrier or American Pit Bull Terrier!*

## Special Considerations for APBT/Amstaff Training

Like socialization, training for an American Pit Bull Terrier or an American Staffordshire Terrier must come early. Experts suggest that training should begin at several months of age for some breeds—but not the APBT/Amstaff. Knowledgeable APBT/Amstaff people assert that for their pets, training must begin at a few weeks of age, not months!

Training these dogs does not have to be quite as repetitive as for some other breeds. When it is apparent that the puppy understands a command, do not overdo the repetitions. A puppy that becomes bored or jaded with a command will stop paying attention and learning actually stops.

## Training an Adopted Adult Dog

Your new adult APBT/Amstaff may have had some rudimentary training. The shelter or rescue organization can tell you what they know on this subject. Follow the basic training outlined here for puppies and your adult dog will soon pick up these basic commands.

As with puppies, never try to train an adult when you are angry or frustrated. Be patient and kind. Take a little extra time and reward appropriately (with food treats for adults).

Most American Pit Bull Terriers and American Staffordshire Terriers are bright and will want to please you. Your real trick is being able to communicate to the dog how to do what you want.

## Pack Behavior and Your APBT/Amstaff

Your American Staffordshire or APBT will be a beloved member of your family. However, you are not your pet's first family affiliation. Your American Pit Bull Terrier or Amstaff is also a pack member, as are wolves and other canines. The pack is the most important part of a dog's life. It is the natural caste system or pecking order that dictates where each and every dog fits in.

Feral dogs will form pack hierarchies identical to that of wolves. The pack has a clearly defined rank-ordering system with each animal at its own level, dominant over those below it on the ladder, subservient to those above it. The leader,

identified as the alpha or first male, is usually the biggest, strongest, most keenly intelligent dog in the pack. All other pack members bend to the will of this leader unless they are ready to challenge him for the top spot.

Pack behavior is something that your APBT/Amstaff will usually already understand when he gets to your home. He learned this concept from his mother and with his mother, siblings, and the breeder, a pack superstructure was already in place. The mother dog is always the leader of her litter pack, but the siblings work out who is next in line and so forth.

### Understanding Pack Hierarchy

Understanding pack behavior is crucial to training your pet. Like using denning behavior in crate training, pack behavior can be used to make certain that your American Pit Bull Terrier or Amstaff knows his place within your family and is content with the arrangement. Within your home setting and throughout the life of your APBT/Amstaff, *you* have to be the dominant leader; *you* have to fill the alpha slot. The other members of your family or household will be the other pack members with the dog fitting in neatly as the *last* one on the list.

The pack is not some power game everyone plays against the dog. Pack membership for a canine is as natural as any other instinctive behavior. It serves as important ballast in the dog's life, providing the security, appropriate rank placement, and sense of belonging that dogs need. A well-adjusted, well-socialized American Pit Bull Terrier or American Staffordshire Terrier needs to understand where he fits in within his social universe. You, or some other responsible human, will have to assume responsibility for seeing that this natural chain of command is instilled in your family and remains in place.

You can observe pack behavior in any grouping of dogs. Two dogs meet for the first time. They stand rather stiff-legged, often going through the sniffing ritual. Unless a fight is imminent, one dog will recognize that he should be subservient to the other. The subservient dog will actually assume submissive demeanor and do submissive things to show he is no threat to the dominant animal. Some of these submissive behaviors are cringing, offering no defense, rolling over on his back, or even releasing small amounts of urine.

## Build on the Mother Dog's Training Model

Training your American Staffordshire or American Pit Bull Terrier will be considerably quicker and easier if you build on the training the puppy's mother has already provided. The model for training that she used is an excellent

one for you to adapt. Following her example will make you a better trainer and your APBT/Amstaff a better pet.

**Fairness:** Each puppy in the litter got equal treatment. No puppy was able to get away with a transgression for which another would be punished. The discipline meted out by the mother was also fair and appropriate for the misdeed.

**Immediacy:** A wayward puppy was disciplined immediately while the youngster's short attention span could still associate the misdeed with the subsequent reprimand.

**Without anger:** The puppies were disciplined without anger. The mother's actions were not designed to injure the puppies, but to mold their behavior. She also did not subject a miscreant puppy to long periods of incessant barking or growling to unsuccessfully correct his behavior.

**Consistency:** The puppies were able to learn from the consistent manner in which their mother acted. A transgression did not receive discipline on one occasion and a reward the next time. The youngsters came to understand that certain misdeeds would bring about certain discipline, each and every time.

**With love:** The puppies were reproved and corrected in a secure and nurturing environ-

ment. An earlier misdeed did not force a puppy into exile. The love of the mother and the support of the littermates were not withheld as additional discipline.

A well-adjusted Amstaff or APBT mother will have built a firm foundation for the future training of her offspring. By following her model of fairness, immediate response, absence of anger, and consistency in a loving environment, you will find your pet much easier to train.

## How Dog Training Works

The mother's example provides humans with insight into how dog training is actually accomplished. Dogs learn by having negative actions corrected and having positive actions rewarded and reinforced. If a puppy jumps up on a couch and gets a firm "*No*" and is gently, but very definitely, removed from that couch, he will soon get the idea that the couch is off-limits. However, if one member of the family lets the puppy get on the couch, he will only become confused and possibly resentful when he is reprimanded and removed.

There are many schools of thought about dog training. These range from harsh methods using slapping and beating to quasi-training that passively allows the dog to do what he wants to do. The mother's model is one constant that most successful approaches have as their center.

## Crate Training

Crate training works because your Amstaff or APBT puppy almost instinctively will not want to mess up his den or sleeping area. The puppy will normally learn this behavior from his mother who would chastise an older puppy

who made a mess in the litter's sleeping quarters. In the wild, canines don't want to let the smell of feces and urine become an attractant for predators. For this reason denning areas are not normally fouled with urine and feces. Crate training takes advantage of two very strong innate behaviors: 1. denning behavior, and 2. the desire to keep a den area clean. By encouraging these behaviors you can make crate training not only convenient and useful for you, but natural and comfortable for your pet. Remember the following things about crate training:

✔ Keep a positive attitude about crates. Knowledgeable dog owners know that the crate is a place of refuge for a puppy or a dog, not a cruel prison.

✔ When you purchase a cage/crate/carrier for your Amstaff or American Pit Bull Terrier, bear in mind that the small puppy of today will be the sturdy, medium-sized dog of the near future. Buy a crate for the *adult dog*. Use temporary partitions, usually available where you buy the crate or easily made, to keep the crate the right size for a growing puppy. If the crate is too large, the puppy may develop a waste elimination area in the corner away from where he sleeps. Keep the crate just big enough for the growing youngster.

✔ Place the crate in an out-of-the-way, but not an isolated, place in your home. This location must be away from highly changeable temperature fluctuations, drafts, and direct sunshine.

✔ Put the puppy in his den when he needs to rest and for a few hours when you will not be around to supervise him. Always take the puppy out of the crate and outside as soon as you return home.

✔ Taking the puppy out of the crate should not become a reward. Do not praise the youngster (except at the relief spot outside) for 10 or 15 minutes after you let him out of the crate.

✔ Make the crate comfortable for the puppy by placing a sleeping mat into the crate. These mats are made to fit every size of cage, crate, or carrier, and come in many washable colors and designs.

✔ Do not put food or water in the crate. This will only promote a messy sleeping area; food and water are best kept elsewhere.

# TIP

### Training

Training hint: Go over with your family what each training session is going to try to teach your puppy. Make sure your family understands that they can confuse and set back the progress of a youngster by doing things that undo the training.

✔ If the youngster whines, barks, or cries in the crate, use a calm, authoritative voice to quiet the puppy (see Helping Your Puppy Settle In, page 37).

✔ Be certain that all members of your household understand what the crate does and what crate training is all about.

✔ While training your pet, return him to the crate for a half-hour break before letting him out for a play session. This will imprint on the puppy that training is serious and not just part of playtime.

## Basic Training

Your American Pit Bull Terrier or American Staffordshire Terrier will need early and consistent training. By remembering that some puppies mature faster than others, you will be able to find a good time to begin a more serious approach to teaching your puppy the basic things he must learn in order to live with a family.

Initially, you will want your American Pit Bull Terrier or Amstaff to learn five basic commands. These commands will give you a good level of control over your young puppy, which is a crucial element to successful dog ownership. These commands are: *sit, stay, heel, down,* and *come.* Each of these commands involves a slightly different level of training. Each will be useful in everyday pet ownership.

# The Essentials of Training Your Puppy

• **Establish a regular training schedule each day.** Training sessions do not have to be long. Between 10 and 15 minutes for each session is sufficient.

• **Keep the sessions geared toward training.** Avoid places and times when there are distractions that could draw away the full attention of your puppy. Although these times should be enjoyable, they are not times for play.

• **Fill the alpha role.** The firm, businesslike sound of your voice will let the puppy know training time is different from playtime and that you are in charge. Be stern and consistent, but remember to never attempt training when you are angry or upset over something.

• **Set clear and attainable training goals.** Before each training session set definite, but reasonable, goals you want to accomplish in this session. Don't expect too much too soon. Make training a matter of small, incremental steps that will ultimately move you and your Amstaff/APBT puppy in a specific direction.

• **Conduct each session as a single-focus class.** You know that your APBT or American Staffordshire Terrier may not respond well to a lot of meaningless repetitive commands. You also know that each session must have a

beginning point and an ending point. Try to end each session in a positive way.

• **Stick to your planned goals for that session.** When you train your puppy, you can go back over previous lessons, but if the goal for today is heeling, focus on heeling. Correct your puppy each time he does not heel correctly and praise him each time he does heel correctly. If your APBT or Amstaff puppy begins to chafe with the repetitions, cut the session short.

• **Reward the right way.** Some animal trainers use small bits of food as a reward during train-

ing; other dog trainers use praise. Many use a combination of both. When working with puppies use what you deem most appropriate. I like to begin with praise and move to small bits of a tasty treat to speed and reinforce training. Training adults should always involve both praise and treat rewards.

• **Separate training time from fun time.** You want to keep your puppy's attention on what he must learn. Put a little distance in the puppy's mind between the training session and any subsequent play. Reward a trainee for doing the right thing; however, wait until later to show lavish affection as you play with your beloved pet.

• **Follow the mother dog's example of correcting immediately.** Like the mother dog, you should make corrections right then, right on the spot. Waiting to correct a puppy later is useless because the youngster may not even remember the misdeed.

• **Consistency, the key to good training.** You may only be an amateur training your first dog, but, if you are consistent, doing the training the same way each time, you will get better results than an experienced professional who is inconsistent. The young dog will need to know that the stern alpha voice you use during training means that this is serious. If you use a different tone or different words in the basic commands, the puppy cannot guess what you want!

• **Patience is the greatest virtue in training.** As important as consistency is, without patience you are lost. Regardless of how good an American Pit Bull Terrier or Amstaff puppy you think you have, he is still just a puppy. Bruiser may want to learn from you to gain your praise, but if you push him faster than he can go you could ruin a fine young animal. Always be patient, both with your pet and with yourself as a trainer.

• **Avoid immediate training sessions after long periods of crate confinement.** Puppies will usually have a lot of pent-up energy at this time and will find concentrating on their lessons difficult.

# The Right Training Equipment

Training equipment for your Amstaff/APBT will consist of the following items:

**A training collar:** Although commonly misnamed a *choke* collar, the training collar is both humane and effective when used correctly and appropriately. This collar is for use *only* during training sessions. When correcting pressure is applied with a very gentle and slight snap, the dog's head will come up and his attention will be brought back to the training. Combined with a stern "*No*," this training collar not only controls and corrects, it lets him know that he did something wrong. This chain collar should be large enough to go over the widest part of your puppy's head with no more than an inch leeway. This collar is, as stated, not for regular wear. The puppy should associate the training collar with the serious business of learning. This chain collar also could become snagged on something and cause the youngster to be injured if he wears it all the time.

**A training leash (or lead):** Along with the training collar, you will need to purchase a 1-inch (2.5-cm)-wide lead (commonly called a leash) that will not be used on your regular walks with your Amstaff or APBT puppy. This lead or leash, like the training collar, is just for training. It should be made of leather, nylon, or

woven web material. It should be 6 feet (1.8 m) long, be of sturdy construction, and have a comfortable and strong hand loop on one end. On the other end should be a brass or stainless steel swivel snap that can be attached to the ring on Bruiser's training collar.

Let your puppy become thoroughly familiar with both the collar and the lead before you actually begin using them. These two items are important tools of the dog trainer's trade and should be of excellent quality. The Amstaff or American Pit Bull Terrier puppy should not fear or dislike these tools. They should signify that training time is here.

# The Five Basic Commands

## Before You Begin Training

Just like a drill sergeant about to train some new soldiers, you need to have a command voice to best get your orders across with the following aspects:

**Firmness:** Give one-word commands in a clear voice to your dog, always using his name before each command to get his attention: "*Bruiser, sit.*" Be firm and businesslike. Don't talk baby talk or use pet nicknames—playtime is later. This is training time.

**Consistency:** Use the same tone of voice each and every time so that your tone as well as your voice will reinforce the seriousness of this training time.

**Be specific—don't issue a string of several commands at one time:** "*Bruiser, come here and sit down*" is a terrible attempt at telling your APBT/Amstaff what you want. This babble will only confuse him. Each command should be a single, specific word pronounced the same way and in the same tone each time.

**Use the mother model:** Remember that the puppy's first training came from a real expert, his mother.

## "Sit"

Because your puppy will already know how to sit, your main role is to teach him when to sit and where to sit. The *sit* is a good first lesson for your puppy to learn because so many other basic and advanced obedience commands begin or end in this natural position.

The training collar should be on the puppy's neck and correctly attached to the leash or lead. Start the *sit* with the youngster on your left, next to your left leg. Take up all but about 12 inches (30 cm) of the excess lead. Hold the lead in your right hand. In a smooth, continuous, gentle, but firm upward move, lift the puppy's head so that he is facing a little above horizontal. As you do so, with your left hand press gently downward on his hindquarters. The lift of his head combined with the pushing down on his hindquarters will force the young dog to sit down as you give the command, *"Bruiser, sit!"*

Be careful not to push down on the puppy's rear end hard enough to injure or frighten the youngster; you want only to make him sit, not hurt him. After the puppy does sit, give him lots of praise and a reward. Just as with voiding waste at the relief spot, you want the puppy to associate the praise/reward with the action. This is the basis of dog training. Do not overdo the first few sessions and don't keep a puppy sitting too long or tire or bore him with too many repetitions. Keep the sessions interesting and enjoyable for the puppy.

## "Stay"

After Bruiser has mastered the *sit*, he is ready for the next command, the *stay*. This command actually begins with your pet in the *sit* and really can't be learned until the *sit* is firmly a part of what he knows.

The *stay* begins with the puppy sitting next to your left leg. The lead is again in your right hand and is used to hold up the head of the youngster. Using your firm, alpha voice, give the command *"Bruiser, stay!"* as you step straight forward away from the sitting puppy, leading with your right foot. At the same time, bring the palm of your left hand down in front of the young dog's face in an upside-down version of the police hand signal for stop.

Some American Staffordshire Terrier or American Pit Bull Terrier puppies will easily

## The *Stay*

The *stay* will require four coordinated parts done at precisely the same time:

**1.** your gentle lifting pressure on the lead to keep the puppy's head up

**2.** your step forward, beginning with your right foot

**3.** your left hand being placed, palm down, in front of the dog's face

**4.** your clear, firm vocal command, *"Bruiser, stay!"*

learn the *stay*, but others will have some trouble with it. If your puppy doesn't stay at first, don't overdo this command the first few *stay*

training sessions. You can try it several times. If the puppy has trouble, go back to a few *sits* and let the puppy end each session with some successes and the praise/reward these successes should always bring.

Patience is needed in teaching a very young dog this conflicting command. Take your time. Remember this is just a young puppy you are working with. Be consistent in how you give the command, pull up on the lead, step away, and put your palm in front of the puppy's face. Your efforts will pay off and your puppy will stay.

The length of the *stay* a puppy executes may not be very long at first, but gradually the puppy will learn to stay where you want him to and you can move farther and farther away. Remember to praise/reward the puppy for any length of stay.

Once the puppy can handle this fairly tough command, you can insert a cheerfully given release word, "*OK*," which will let Bruiser know that he can do what he really wants to—come to you and be rewarded.

## "Heel"

Being able to walk with your pet at the correct place by your left leg will be a useful thing for a young puppy to know. The *heel* takes on added importance with the American Pit Bull Terrier and the Amstaff because these dogs can often be real pullers. Teaching a very young APBT or American Staffordshire not to attempt to drag you along behind him is a crucially important skill. You will be able to control the pulling and tugging of a little dog (which is a bad dominance testing habit), but a 60-pound (27.2-kg) dog can probably tow all children and many adults. The time to teach the *heel* is while you still have the upper hand and are stronger and higher on the pack ladder than your terrier.

Like the *stay*, the *heel* begins in the *sit* position. Both the *sit* and the *stay* must be mastered by him before you should attempt to teach heeling. Hold the lead, still attached to the training collar, in your right hand. The puppy should be sitting alongside your left foot. As you give the clear, alpha-voiced command, *"Bruiser, heel!"* step off, leading with your left foot this time. If the puppy doesn't move forward when you do, pop the leftover loop of the lead loudly against the side of your left leg and keep on walking. The absence of your palm in his face plus your movement with the left foot rather than the right, combined with the gentle forward pull of the lead on the collar, should cause Bruiser to move along with you.

When the puppy starts walking with you, praise him, but keep on moving. Keep praising and rewarding Bruiser as long as he stays with you, right by your left side. If he has problems with this command, do not drag him all over the yard attempting to get him moving. Start the *heel* lesson again by going back to the *sit* and *stay* positions and following the steps of the command:

When you stop, give the *sit* command—the puppy will want to walk along with you. Since the *heel* makes this possible it should be fairly easy for Bruiser to learn. Teach the *heel* the right way each time, correcting the puppy immediately if he tries to lag behind you, branch off in another direction, or run on ahead of you. You have to be the one who will choose where you walk and how fast you will go. As with other lessons, make this enjoyable, but be consistent and patient.

## "Down"

The *down* command also has its beginnings with the *sit* and the *stay*. It has some aspects of the *stay* in that you want the puppy to remain in this one spot. It is different than the *stay* in that you use downward pressure on the lead, this time with your left hand, instead of upward pressure. You want Bruiser's head and torso to go downward and for him to lie on his stomach.

With your right hand, pull down on the lead while making a strong, repeated downward motion (not unlike slowly bouncing a basketball) in front of the dog's face. At the same time you do these two things, give the clear, firm command using the dog's name, as in *"Bruiser, down!"*

## TIP

### Come Command

Don't use the *come* command too much as the puppy could become bored or lax at performing numerous repetitions of it. One good way to use it is to surprise the puppy when he is doing something else—playing or running in the backyard. Give the *come* command when the youngster isn't expecting it and then heap on the praise/reward for quick obedience.

When the puppy has reached the belly-on-the-ground position, heap on the praise and reward. The *down* is made easier because it is a natural position that he already knows. Your role is to teach him to do the *down* when you command him to do so. The constant, but gentle, downward pull of the lead in your hand will force Bruiser to comply with your wishes.

The *down* is another command that must be taught to the APBT/Amstaff while you still have the leverage and greater power to teach it. It is possible that you could have more difficulty teaching the *down* to an adult American Staffordshire or American Pit Bull Terrier that really did not want to do it. Start young to make this command as automatic as possible.

### "Come"

All dogs know how to come to their master or mistress, don't they? This may be true when the dog himself wants to come to you, but the *come* command is very important in that it stresses that Bruiser is to come to you, each and every time you give the command.

Along with patience and consistency, the *come* will require enthusiasm from you. You should always call the dog by name, *"Bruiser, come!"* When beginning your teaching of this command, let cheerfulness blend with your firmness of voice. Make this command to a very young puppy an invitation to join the person he loves. Spread your arms out wide and call the puppy to you, using the appropriate command. When the youngster does what he really wants to do anyway—that is come to be with you—give him a lot of praise.

The *come* can be misused and a puppy or dog actually taught to ignore the command. *Never* call your APBT/Amstaff to you to discipline him, reprimand him, or to do anything that may be perceived by the youngster as negative! Never allow anyone in your household to do this. The puppy must associate the command to come with a happy outcome when he obeys, not with the possibility that he will be punished or scolded for something. As you should never scold or reprimand a puppy or dog at the special waste relief site, you should never use the *come* to get the animal within reach so you can do something he will not like. If you need to punish or reprimand, *go to the dog*; do not try to make him come to you.

One way to teach the *come* to a young and possibly inattentive puppy is by using the regular lead, or even a longer training lead of 20 feet (6.1 m) or more, attached to the training collar. Exert gentle pressure in bringing him toward you combined with the happy, enthusiastic *come* command with the lavish praise/reward for him when he obeys.

## Obedience Classes to Help You *AND* Your Dog

Although your training efforts will normally be sufficient, you should avail yourself of any dog-training classes that are in your area. Not only will you and Bruiser learn more quickly, you will do so with experienced trainers who have dealt with any problems that may arise for you and the dog. These training classes are usually held in the evenings or weekends at some easily accessible place. They have much to offer you and your American Staffordshire or American Pit Bull Terrier.

Your puppy will gain socialization skills by being around other humans who like and understand young dogs. Bruiser will get exposure to other dogs that are there for the same training. This will give you a chance to observe, under tightly controlled conditions, the level of animal aggressive tendencies your young APBT/Amstaff may have. This is an extremely valuable piece of information for you to have!

## Crate Training

Crate training will play the role it does in housetraining when you know when your puppy will most need to void. You should plan trips to the relief area right after the puppy drinks some water or eats some puppy food. The additional pressure on his bladder or colon will require a trip outside. In addition, follow these suggestions to help your puppy:

✔ Plan a trip there after periods of prolonged active play.

✔ Take the puppy out of his crate and go to the relief spot as late at night as possible.

✔ Take the puppy out as early in the morning as you can.

✔ Although very late or early trips may become less necessary as the puppy grows up, plan on relief breaks several times a day whenever you and Bruiser are together.

✔ Recognize the telltale signs that a puppy or dog may give when an outside trip is needed:

**1.** A general look of discomfort or anxiety on the dog's face.

**2.** Circling in one spot as if looking for a clue where to go.

**3.** Staying near the door to the outside area.

**4.** Whining and whimpering and running toward the door to get your attention.

**5.** Going into a squatting posture.

✔ If Bruiser cannot wait, gently, calmly, but quickly, pick him up and go to the relief spot even if he has an accident. At the relief spot wait until he eliminates there and then praise him enthusiastically.

✔ Thoroughly clean any soiled spots and make use of scent neutralizers ("Nature's Miracle" and similar products), as canines are motivated to use a spot where the smell of previous urine or feces remains.

✔ *Never* speak harshly or reprimand the puppy at the relief spot for any reason. This is a place where Bruiser needs lots of little victories and rewards of praise from you. Don't confuse the youngster with correction at this special site.

✔ *Never* rub a puppy's nose in his messes. This stupid behavior on your part does nothing positive for the puppy's learning and only gets him dirty.

✔ *Never* strike a puppy with your hand, a rolled up newspaper, or anything else! This

*Great aids to housetraining your puppy are automatic outside visits after eating or drinking, late at night, and first thing in the morning.*

especially applies to a natural activity like defecating or urinating. This will only make the puppy fear you and will actually slow down learning.

✔ Screaming at a puppy in the act of making a mess in the house is futile. You might gain some time to get the youngster outside by clapping your hands and saying a firm "*No*," which may break his concentration on making a mess. Rush the puppy outside and praise him when he goes where he should.

✔ Feed a high-quality, dry puppy food that provides excellent digestibility. The stools with this kind of food will generally be smaller and firmer—an added benefit if an accident does happen and easier for the puppy to retain, thereby decreasing accidents.

✔ Avoid snacks and table scraps. These items will not only unbalance the puppy's diet, but will hinder your effort to time when trips outside should occur.

✔ Don't leave food in the Amstaff or APBT puppy's food bowl all day. This will also throw off your relief trip schedule and puppies generally do better on several small meals each day.

✔ Don't put food or edible toys such as dog biscuits in the crate. Let the crate be a place of rest and/or confinement and have somewhere else for food.

✔ Don't leave your American Pit Bull Terrier or Amstaff puppy in his crate too long as this will be painful for the youngster that may try to

*A puppy sniffing and circling is probably about to eliminate. Watch for this behavior and hurry the puppy outside.*

keep from voiding waste in order to keep the den area clean.

✔ Be consistent with your housetraining efforts and see that others in your household are also. Consistent training will teach most American Staffordshires or APBTs what housetraining is all about.

✔ If you have a fenced backyard, never just turn a puppy out alone to relieve himself. You need to be there to reinforce him (with praise and/or a reward) for going at the right place and the right time.

✔ Playtime should not begin outside until the puppy has used the relief area. Going outside must signify waste relief and not play to the youngster.

For another option, see Paper Training, page 52.

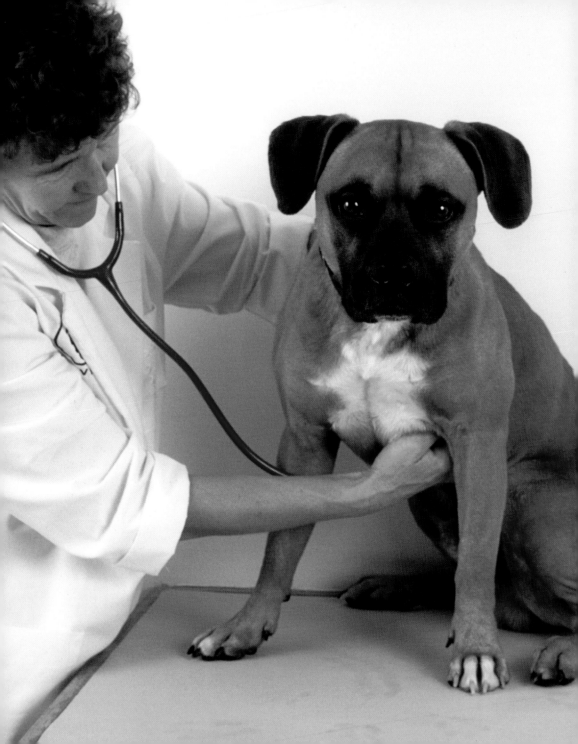

# MEDICAL CARE

*A wide variety of health issues and concerns will normally affect any puppy or adopted adult. A good Amstaff/APBT owner is an alert and aware Amstaff/APBT owner. Know what can harm your pet and how best to prevent it or deal with it.*

## Developing a Wellness Plan for Your Pet

Your Amstaff/APBT will deserve a carefully considered plan to keep him in good shape and let him live out his natural life span. Do not leave the health of this trusting canine member of your family to chance. Concentrate on discovering those things that can harm your pet and then eliminate or deal with them. You may not be able to do this without the help of some other knowledgeable people.

## A Health Care Team

The American Pit Bull Terrier or Amstaff that you have invited into your home will greatly benefit from a group of concerned humans who have his best health interests at heart.

✔ You, and the members of your family, will make up Bruiser's health care team and will be the first line of defense for your puppy in so many areas.

✔ Your veterinarian will be the fulcrum on which the health of your American Staffordshire Terrier or American Pit Bull Terrier may balance. Find a veterinarian who knows and likes these dogs, and has some experience with them. (This should not be hard as veterinarians are often some of the staunchest supporters of the APBT/Amstaff.) Depend on this professional's expertise in immunization, health problem prevention, and treatment. Follow the suggestions, prescription instructions, and treatment plans worked out by your veterinarian.

✔ Perhaps an experienced APBT/Amstaff person (even by phone or the Internet) could help you with generalized illnesses or conditions affecting these breeds.

# Preventing Accidents

Much of the preventive focus depends on common sense, anticipating problems, and heading off problems. Puppy-proofing is one form of accident prevention. Keeping your APBT/Amstaff under the control of sturdy fencing, strong leashes and collars, and good training is another way to stop accidents before they happen. Spaying and neutering your Amstaffs and American Pit Bull Terriers can be accident prevention, in several senses of the term.

Keeping your terrier out of potentially dangerous spots (like a parked car on a warm day or running off-leash in a city park) is definitely accident prevention. Recognizing that animal aggression is part of the genetic makeup of some Amstaffs or APBTs and dealing with this before problems occur is also in this category.

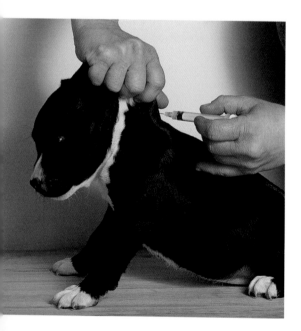

Recognizing that dogs of these two breeds tend to drown more often than do many other breeds can lead an owner to prevent this senseless type of fatality. Protecting your Amstaff/APBT puppy or adult from becoming poisoned from common household sources is good accident prevention.

# Preventing Illnesses

Your American Pit Bull Terrier or American Staffordshire Terrier is an extremely short-coated breed and may suffer from cold weather more acutely than some other breeds. Protect your pet from cold temperatures by letting him live indoors with you. If, at times, he must stay briefly in an outside kennel, provide a thoroughly insulated and draft-proof doghouse.

You and your veterinarian can help eliminate much in the way of parasites and, in so doing, eliminate some of the health problems that can stem from flea, tick, and worm infestation. You can do your part at home by keeping your pet away from unhygienic conditions and away from stray animals that may harbor communicable illnesses.

# Immunizations

Getting your Amstaff or APBT immunized against the wide spectrum of illnesses that attack canines is a key part of your wellness plan for your pet. In some cases, these shots are not options but are mandated by law.

Your American Staffordshire Terrier or APBT may have had his first immunizations when he was about six weeks old. These shots may have been administered while the puppy was still under the breeder's care. You should

have a clearly annotated record of just what shots your new pet had at that time. The first round of immunizations were vaccinations for distemper and possibly for parvovirus, canine hepatitis, leptospirosis, parainfluenza, and coronavirus.

Even if your youngster was immunized for all these illnesses he will still need follow-up shots at eight to ten weeks and again at 12 weeks. Normally the puppy immunizations end with another group of shots at 16 to 18 weeks.

When you take your new puppy to the veterinarian for the first time, take along his medical record that the breeder should have supplied. Your dog's doctor will need to know what immunizations and other treatments this puppy may have received. Take care of these early documents as they form the nucleus of what should be your pet's lifelong health records.

When your veterinarian sets up an immunization schedule for your young APBT or American Staffordshire, follow it with the greatest of care. The best puppy from the best breeder can die amazingly quickly if you have not been diligent in getting immunizations done at the recommended times.

# Common Ailments in the APBT/Amstaff

### Distemper

One of the oldest enemies of the canine, wild and domestic, is distemper. At one time, this widespread and extremely infectious viral killer was the greatest known threat to puppies and young dogs. Entire kennels were wiped out by distemper.

Today there is an immunization program that has greatly decreased the incidence of distemper. Distemper, although more controlled now than decades ago, is still deadly when animals have not been immunized against it. Distemper is still very much in evidence among wild canines and in places where vaccination for it is inadequate or nonexistent.

A dog not completely immunized against distemper may show clinical signs as early as a week after being near an animal with the disease. At first, distemper looks like a cold with a runny nose accompanied by a slight fever. Dogs will often stop eating and exhibit fatigue, listlessness, and diarrhea.

## Rabies

Rabies is one of those diseases that bring about nightmares of loving pets transformed into vicious, foaming-at-the-mouth canine demons bent on biting any and everything around them. Rabies is made all the more frightening because it can be transmitted to humans and to most other warm-blooded mammals by the saliva of an infected animal, which is usually passed by a bite. In 1885 French scientist Louis Pasteur developed a vaccine for this dreaded disease. Until Pasteur, rabies meant certain death in the most hideous manner imaginable!

**Symptoms:** One of the classic indicators of rabies was supposed to be the other name by which this dreaded killer is known—hydrophobia, or fear of water. Paralysis of the laryngeal muscles that control swallowing brings on excessive salivation or foaming at the mouth. The dog does not fear water as much as he is unable to drink and swallow.

Rabies in companion animals is fairly uncommon now due to an aggressive immunization plan. It still occurs in populations of wild animals, skunks, raccoons, foxes, and stray or feral dogs and cats.

**Stages:** Rabies has two stages or phases. The first, often called the *furious* phase, is so named because the inflicted animal may attack anything with which it comes in contact. Some animals die while still in the furious mode, but others live to go into the second phase. This is often called the *dumb* phase, which ultimately ends in paralysis, unconsciousness, and finally death.

Failure to keep a dog immunized against such an infectious and horrible killer is negligent and unlawful. Protect your puppy, your family, and yourself by making certain that your puppy gets immunized at four months of age. Also be sure that your pet gets his second shot at about sixteen months of age (one year after the initial shot) with annual to triennial shots for the rest of his life!

## Leptospirosis

Leptospirosis is a bacterial disease that primarily does damage to the infected dog's kidneys. In advanced cases, it can severely injure both the liver and the kidneys, causing jaundice, sores in the dog's mouth, a loss in weight, and a general weakening of the dog's hindquarters.

Leptospirosis is commonly spread by drinking water contaminated by an animal with the disease. Clinical signs of this illness are loss of appetite, fever, diarrhea, abdominal pain, and vomiting. Immunization followed by an annual booster shot will protect your pet from leptospirosis. Vaccination for leptospirosis does not prevent a dog from becoming a carrier of the disease and a potential transmitter of the disease to humans.

## Hepatitis

Infectious canine hepatitis is not the same illness that humans can contract. The canine version can affect any member of the Canis family and can range in severity from a deadly viral infection that can kill a dog within one day's time after it is diagnosed, to a fairly mild disease.

This infectious disease can be spread by coming in contact with the urine or feces of a dog inflicted with infectious canine hepatitis. Clinical signs of the illness are listlessness, abdominal pain, tonsillitis, increased light sensitivity, fever, and bloody stools and/or vomitus.

Infectious canine hepatitis can be prevented by a good immunization program followed up by annual boosters.

## Parvovirus

Young puppies especially fall victim to parvovirus, but this viral disease can take the life of an unimmunized dog at any age! Parvovirus primarily attacks the immune system, gastrointestinal tract, and heart, along with the bone marrow. Young animals with this disease can suffer severe dehydration due to profuse bloody and watery diarrhea and vomiting. From the onset of the disease, parvovirus can kill an affected dog or puppy within 48 hours.

Immediate medical care can save some parvovirus-stricken dogs and puppies from death. However, an effective immunization program can spare most from ever contracting the disease. Annual boosters should follow a puppy vaccination for parvovirus.

## Parainfluenza

This highly contagious virus can spread rapidly through a litter of puppies or through a

home with several dogs. Parainfluenza is thought to be spread by contact with infected animals, as well as through the air. This disease causes tracheobronchitis (sometimes accompanied by *bordetella*), which causes a dry, hacking cough followed by repeated attempts to cough up mucus.

Parainfluenza alone is not usually very serious. If tracheobronchitis is left untreated, it can sufficiently weaken a victim and leave it vulnerable to other infections. The best course of action with parainfluenza is immunization in the puppy series of shots followed by annual reinforcement by booster.

A dog or puppy with parainfluenza is usually treated by a veterinarian in isolated conditions to prevent the spread of this disease.

be successfully treated, but prevention through immunization is again the best course.

## Borelliosis (Lyme Disease)

Borelliosis, or Lyme disease, affects many mammals including humans. It is a serious, potentially fatal illness that is believed to be spread primarily by the tiny deer tick to dogs or to dog owners.

Although originally identified in and named for Lyme, Connecticut, this disease, which carries the medical name of borelliosis, has now spread to many parts of the United States. At one time, only hunters and hunting dogs were considered prime candidates to be infected. However, you or your dog could contract this ailment in a city park or even in a suburban backyard.

**Signs:** Clinical signs of Lyme disease include swelling and tenderness around joints, and a loss of appetite. If you or your APBT/Amstaff have been bitten by any tick, you would be wise to seek a professional medical and veterinary opinion as soon as possible! Fortunately a vaccine now exists for Lyme disease.

# Other Possible Health Problems

## Anal Gland Impaction

On either side of a dog's anus lie the anal sacs. Normal defecation usually empties these sacs but sometimes they become clogged or impacted. When impaction occurs, these sacs must be emptied of their strong-smelling secretions by hand.

One sure sign of anal sac impaction is the scooting motion seen in an affected dog as

## Coronavirus

Both puppies and adult dogs of all ages can become victims of coronavirus. This contagious disease, which is characterized by severe diarrhea with loose, foul-smelling, watery stools tinged with blood, can rapidly debilitate a dog or puppy. In a condition weakened by coronavirus, an afflicted animal can contract parvovirus or other infections. An Amstaff or American Pit Bull Terrier with coronavirus can

he drags his rear end along the floor. Your veterinarian can handle this concern, or you can easily learn to do it yourself.

## Diarrhea

Some diarrhea is common in dogs and puppies. It may be caused by stress, food changes, or internal parasites. Diarrhea can also signal the onset of some serious illness. Any diarrhea that continues for more than 12 to 24 hours should alert you to the need for a trip with your pet to the veterinarian.

## Vomiting

Like diarrhea, some vomiting is to be expected. Excitement in puppies after eating may bring it on. A change in diet or added stress may also cause vomiting.

Also like diarrhea, vomiting can be a signal that something more serious may be happening within your dog or puppy. Vomiting and diarrhea can lead to dehydration, which can put a young puppy's life in peril rather quickly. Any vomiting that continues over an extended period (more than 12 hours) should trigger an automatic visit to the veterinary clinic.

## Bloat (Gastric Torsion)

Bloat, or gastric torsion, is a very serious health concern for all deep-chested breeds of dogs, which includes the American Staffordshire Terrier and the American Pit Bull Terrier. Bloat can painfully kill an otherwise healthy dog in just a few hours. It involves a swelling and torsion (or twisting) of the dog's stomach from water or gas or both.

Bloat is still somewhat of a mysterious ailment. There are a lot of suggested causes that may work independently of each other or that may combine to cause bloating. Some of these include the following:

✔ A large meal, particularly of dry dog food, followed by a large intake of water, followed by strenuous exercise.

✔ A genetic predisposition in some breeds and even within some strains or families within a breed.

✔ Stress from any of several sources.

✔ The age of the dog. Dogs over 24 months old seem to be more likely to bloat than do younger animals.

✔ The gender of a dog. Males seem to be more affected by bloat than are females.

From whatever cause, bloat is a real killer of deep-chested dogs. Although the American Pit Bull Terrier and the Amstaff are apparently not quite as susceptible as Bloodhounds, Great Danes, and some others, enough APBTs and Amstaffs die from bloat to make it something you will want to know about. Some clinical signs of bloat include the following:

• Obvious abdominal pain and noticeable abdominal swelling.

• Excessive salivation and rapid breathing.

• Pale and cool-to-the-touch skin in the mouth.

• A dazed and shocked look.

• Multiple attempts to vomit, especially when nothing comes up.

A dog with bloat needs super-immediate care if he is to stand a chance of survival. First, alert your veterinarian; then safely transport your dog to the clinic.

## Canine Hip Dysplasia

One of the most discussed and problematic canine health issues for modern dog owners is CHD, or canine hip dysplasia. CHD does not have the life-threatening immediacy of many of the common canine diseases or of gastric torsion (bloat), but it can be quite debilitating and painful for a dog that has a severe form of this condition.

By description, CHD is a medical condition in which the hip joint is slack or loose. This slackness or looseness is combined with a deformity of the socket of the hip and the femoral head joining the thighbone. This malformation of the development of the hip's bone and connective tissues leaves an unstable hip joint. Instead of a strong fit like a cup for the end of the thighbone, the CHD-affected hip is often quite shallow. This condition can cause an unsteady, wobbling gait that can be very painful.

Much has been written about the possibility of CHD being an inherited disorder. This may be only partially accurate, for not every puppy born of a dysplastic sire and/or dam will have the condition. It is conversely also true that even normal or non-CHD parents can produce some dysplastic offspring.

CHD cannot be determined with any degree of certainty until a dog is around two years old. The Orthopedic Foundation for Animals (OFA) has developed a widely used X-ray process that is used to determine if CHD is present in a dog and the degree to which it is present. Some veterinarians may also be able to pre-screen for CHD by using the Penn hip testing method on younger dogs.

American Staffordshire Terriers are fairly high on the list of breeds that have a relatively high incidence of hip dysplasia. The better the CHD test scores on your puppy's parents, the better your chances seem to be of getting a youngster that won't be crippled by this painful condition. CHD is just another reason for taking your time

when you set out to find the right American Pit Bull Terrier or American Staffordshire Terrier puppy.

## Allergies, Skin, and Coat Problems

Some dogs in every breed seem to become the victim of every allergy and skin or coat problem that comes along. The presence of inherited conditions is something that you will want to avoid in the puppy of your choice. One reason for seeing the parents of your puppy is to personally assess their appearance. Other than the wear and tear that you should expect on the coat of a brood bitch that has just gone through pregnancy and puppy raising, the parents should look good.

There are some colors within the American Pit Bull Terrier and American Staffordshire Terrier breeds that may tend to have more skin problems than others. It is thought that the dilute colors—blue, chocolate (or liver), and cream—may be more susceptible to skin worries than others. This is not always the case, but dilute colors do, in all breeds where they occur, tend to prove out this hypothesis.

What you feed your pet may contribute to the presence of skin conditions. Some ingredients are said to produce rashes or "hot spots" in some dogs and even in some breeds.

Washing your APBT or Amstaff too often will promote a dry coat and flaky skin. It is also true that poor housing and poorly maintained hygiene can contribute to skin problems. Stress and allergies to common household chemicals can cause skin and coat problems.

By and large, most American Pit Bull Terriers and most American Staffordshire Terriers are not plagued with the high percentages of allergic reactions and poor skin and coats with which some other breeds must contend. Choosing the right breeder and the right stock from which to choose your puppy will usually help you avoid most inherited skin concerns.

Some APBTs and Amstaffs will have severe reactions to insect bites. Bee stings and ant bites can cause excessive swelling and possible death for some dogs. Watch for these reactions and rush your pet to the veterinarian.

## Inherited Conditions

Because much of their fairly recent history involved the necessity for superb physical conditioning, both the American Staffordshire Terrier and the American Pit Bull Terrier do not have much of a legacy of poor inheritance. Their ancestry had to survive under the toughest of circumstances; therefore, these breeds did not, until the recent flush of popularity, have poor-quality specimens serving as breeding stock.

Some closely bred (line-bred or inbred) strains or families may be more prone to some inherited problems. As mentioned, some families may tend to be more animal aggressive than others. This trait, which was highly desired during the "pit" days, must still be considered an inherited condition. This, and other isolated family traits and inheritances, would almost be from strain to strain rather than representative of these breeds as a whole. Your breeder would be the best source of information about inherited traits and behaviors, good or bad, in the ancestry of the puppy that you choose.

Your veterinarian is a good resource in helping to identify clinical signs of some inherited condition that may exist within your adopted American Staffordshire Terrier or American Pit Bull Terrier. Issues such as Canine Hip Dysplasia

(CHD), Progressive Retinal Atrophy, and Cerebellar Ataxia in both American Staffordshire Terriers and APBTs should definitely be investigated in many older dogs.

# Parasites

## Internal Parasites

Worms sap the vitality out of young and older dogs alike. Your veterinarian can help prevent these pests from inflicting their damage on your APBT/Amstaff. Good hygiene in your home can help eliminate much of this problem.

**Roundworms:** Roundworms can infest dogs of all ages even though puppies are most often the victims of this internal pest. The puppies often have roundworms even before they are born, having gotten them from their mother prenatally. You may discover roundworms in your puppy's stool or vomitus. Seek immediate professional treatment. Roundworms can be transferred to humans.

**Hookworms:** Hookworms, like roundworms, can be in evidence in dogs throughout their lives. Hookworms are also especially hard on puppies, who simply will not thrive while these worms are in them. Puppies with hookworms will have bloody stools or their feces will appear very dark and tarlike. Puppies with hookworms will sometimes become anemic

and these parasites will reduce a puppy's ability to fight off disease.

**Tapeworms:** Tapeworms are a parasite brought by a parasite. Fleas are the host of tapeworms. When your dog has fleas, he can also have tapeworms. Your Amstaff or APBT will never be at his best while infested with tapeworms. Keep fleas off your dog and out of his environment and then get tapeworms out of your dog.

Your veterinarian will be able to help you dispose of both parasitic problems, the fleas and the tapeworms. Because tapeworms can really hamper a puppy's growth and a dog's potential, get them and any other internal parasites treated as soon as possible.

**Heartworms:** The heartworm is another parasite that comes to you compliments of a pest.

Heartworms are transmitted to your pet through infected mosquitoes. The mosquito bites your pet and deposits heartworm larvae into his tissue. Once in the dog's tissue and ultimately his bloodstream, the maturing larvae will ultimately make their way to the dog's heart. Once there, they will continue to grow and increasingly clog this crucial organ until your pet is fatally affected.

Heartworms have expanded their territory thanks to their mosquito hosts. Today a large part of the United States is threatened by heartworm infestation. The diagnosis for heartworms is made using a blood test. Your veterinarian will help you devise a plan to prevent heartworms from infesting your APBT or Amstaff or in treating an affected animal. The preventive plan will involve regular preventive testing and regular doses of preventive medicine that will kill heartworm larvae before they can enter the dog's heart.

Dogs with heartworms can be treated, but this is a risky, long, and expensive procedure. Prevention of heartworm problems is best for you and best for your dog!

## External Parasites

**Fleas:** Fleas are the curse of many dogs' lives. They are the most common parasite affecting dogs and they literally feed on your dog's blood. In very severe infestations, fleas can cause anemic conditions in canines. Anemia could lead to death, especially in puppies. Fleas add insult to injury in that they are also the host and introducer of tapeworms into dogs.

Some dogs, like some humans, can have a severe allergic reaction to these pests. This flea-bite allergy can cause severe scratching, hair loss, and absolute misery to the afflicted dog. This condition requires immediate treatment by a veterinarian to diagnose and treat the allergy. The owner will have to be absolutely fanatical about ridding the dog's living area of all fleas.

Consult with your veterinarian and with a knowledgeable pet products person to discover the weapons at your disposal to wipe fleas from the face of your dog's world. Flea dips, shampoos, collars, dusts, and sprays are on-dog weapons. Foggers, carpet cleaners, and in-home sprays take care of the dwelling. Yard sprays and kennel dust will stop the fleas that lie in wait outside the home. Be sure to remember to treat those places where the dog may go only sometimes: the car, or the cottage at the lake.

Fleas spend 90 percent of their life cycle OFF your dog. Only the adult fleas, about 10 percent of the flea population, are actually on your pet. Deal with the 90 percent by using products designed for each area (always use great care and always follow the directions!). Your regular exterminator may also be able to help in large areas such as your home and yard.

**Ticks:** Ticks are usually much larger than fleas and they can siphon off just that much more blood. Ticks will fill up on your dog's

## TIP

### Ticks

These pesky parasites are not only a general nuisance; they can carry the life-threatening Lyme disease (see Borelliosis, page 78) and other diseases, such as Rocky Mountain spotted fever, that can affect dogs or humans. Ticks can readily move from your dog, to your children, to you.

will keep them from getting back on your pet later.

**Ear mites:** Your Amstaff or American Pit Bull Terrier's ears can become the target of another external parasite, the ear mite. These microscopic pests live both in the ear and in the ear canal. You can spot their presence there by a dirty, waxy, dark residue on the skin inside the ear.

Ear mites can cause your dog a lot of discomfort. If you see your pet shaking his head from side to side in a violent manner, or if your dog constantly digs at or scratches at his ears, ear mites are possibly to blame.

Although there are home remedies that can stop these mites, always follow your veterinarian's preferred method of handling them. As you look for ticks in your American Staffordshire Terrier's or APBT's ears, look for evidence of ear mites.

**Mange:** There are two kinds of mange. Both are caused by a mite:

✔ Demodectic, or red, mange especially affects puppies and old dogs. Both of these ages are especially susceptible to the ragged and patchy appearance, especially around the head and face, that is commonly called mangy. Red mange can also cause severe hair loss and severe itching.

✔ Sarcoptic mange is also caused by a mite. This one burrows into your dog's skin. It too can cause significant hair loss and intense scratching, which can make unsightly raw wounds on a dog's skin that can become infected. Sarcoptic mange mites can also live temporarily on humans.

Your veterinarian can provide a treatment plan for both kinds of mange and keep your pet from the ugly, uncomfortable, and unhealthy side effects of these tiny mites.

blood and will grow several times their original size. Their bites on a short-haired dog such as the APBT and Amstaff can become unsightly scars. Tick bites also can become infected.

Fortunately, ticks don't seem to be the tough foe that fleas are. They can usually be controlled by the regular use of veterinary-recommended sprays, dips, powders, and flea and tick collars for on-dog use. You may also want to treat the living area with an antitick spray that

# Emergency Care

## Accidents

Do everything you can to prevent accidents, but know that even the best dog owner cannot anticipate every situation in which an accident could occur. The primary rule in trying to help an injured pet is *do not make things worse!* You could get bitten yourself if you carelessly approach even a trusted pet who is confused, in pain, and frightened. If you are injured, that will delay the help you need to get for your dog. Your first step is to find some way to muzzle and immobilize your pet so that he won't hurt you or himself.

Don't be in too much of a rush to move a nonmoving pet. Rough treatment can cause a relatively minor injury to become a severe or even fatal injury. Think clearly and remember that you are your pet's best hope only if you are acting rationally.

If your Amstaff or American Pit Bull Terrier is involved in a fight, remember that these breeds are more likely to make use of their powerful jaws to grab on, hold on, and shake the opponent. If the other dog is some breed or mixture other than an Amstaff or an APBT, you are far more likely to be bitten by the other dog as you try to separate the fighters than by your dog!

## Heatstroke

The most ludicrous way for a dog to die is for its owner to leave him in a parked car on a day when the outside temperature is 60°F (15.6°C).

The metal of the car and the heat-increasing properties of auto glass can turn the family sedan into an oven of death for a pet left there for even a few minutes!

Clinical signs of heatstroke include a dazed look and rapid, shallow panting with a high fever. The dog's gums will be bright red.

Speed is crucial if a dog is in this condition. Act *immediately*. Lower your pet's temperature by pouring a mixture of cool water and rubbing alcohol all over the dog's body, and then take him to the nearest veterinarian!

## Bleeding

The first thing to do when a dog is bleeding is to identify the source of the bleeding. After you are sure that you have the source and not just a bloody spot, apply firm, but gentle, pressure to the wound with your hand. If the wound is on an extremity (front legs, back legs, tail), place a tourniquet between the injury and the dog's heart. Loosen the tourniquet for 30 to 60 seconds every 15 minutes. If the bleeding continues, or if there is significant blood loss, or if it is a gaping wound, your veterinarian should be consulted as soon as possible!

## Poisons

Your American Pit Bull Terrier or American Staffordshire Terrier can be hurt in many ways, but one of the riskiest places is right in your home. Modern life provides many opportunities for a pet to ingest some deadly drug or chemical:

✔ Antifreeze is deadly to dogs and has a sweet taste that attracts them. Spilled or leaked antifreeze may be hard to spot, but your pet can find it.

✔ Chocolate can kill a dog or puppy if eaten in sufficient quantity.

✔ A number of yard and garden plants are dangerous to pets, especially to young puppies that enjoy chewing on things. Favorites such as

# CHECKLIST

## Helping an Injured Pet

✔ Remain calm yourself. Your pet will pick up on your anxiety, if you let it show.

✔ Speak to the pet in a calm, confident voice to reassure him that you are here to take the hurt away. Your dog will usually have confidence in you that you can make things all right.

✔ Move very slowly, with no sudden moves that could alarm an injured and frightened animal.

✔ Even if this dog is your lifelong pal, muzzle him gently, but securely. An APBT- or Amstaff-sized muzzle (available at your pet products store) might be a good investment just in case of injuries, but a necktie, leash, or belt might also work.

✔ After the dog is muzzled, immediately attend to any bleeding (see Bleeding, page 85).

✔ Be very supportive when you try to move an adult American Staffordshire or American Pit Bull Terrier. If you can get someone else to help you, certainly do so. If you can get something, such as a door or wide board, to serve as a safe and secure stretcher, use it.

✔ If you are alone, you may have to use your coat, a piece of carpet, or a tarp to devise a way for you to safely move your pet, gently sliding the dog along if you cannot, or if it is not advisable to, lift him.

✔ Call your veterinarian, or have someone else do it, to alert the clinic of the injury and of your arrival time.

✔ Drive *safely* to the veterinarian. You are more likely to make things worse by driving recklessly.

✔ Follow the age-old medical precept "First, do no harm" in all of your actions designed to help an injured pet.

azalea, rhododendron, and holly can bring death to a young dog. Wild plants such as mistletoe and poison ivy can cause severe, even fatal, reactions in some dogs. Check with your local county extension service for a list of poisonous plants that thrive where you live.

✔ Houseplants such as dieffenbachia, poinsettia, and jade plants can all be killers. Ask your extension service about a list of local favorites and check out any houseplant's poison potential before you bring it into your home.

✔ Keep all insecticides, pesticides, garden and lawn chemicals, and cleaning solvents away from places your Amstaff or APBT can prowl.

If your dog suddenly becomes listless, convulses, seems disoriented, or is unconscious, he may be a victim of poison. Other signs of poison ingestion include a change in color of the mucous membranes, vomiting, and diarrhea. The presence of these signs is worth a trip to the veterinarian that may save the life of your pet!

# Areas Requiring Lifelong Attention

## Teeth

Your APBT or Amstaff will depend greatly on his teeth all his life. These dogs put even greater pressure on their teeth than do some other breeds. Unless you pay close attention to your dog's teeth beginning when he is very young, teeth problems could become a source of pain, discomfort, unpleasant breath, or even life-threatening infections. Dental care for dogs can't just be turned over to your veterinarian during your twice-yearly, regular visits. As with humans, the care of your Amstaff or APBT's mouth, gums, and teeth should be a daily activity.

## Caring for Your Dog's Teeth

✔ Regular inspections will alert you to any abnormalities. Every day, as you pet or play with your American Pit Bull Terrier or American Staffordshire Terrier, take just a moment to settle him down to look at his mouth.

✔ Look at the teeth, gums, throat, and lips not just for tooth decay, but for the presence of tartar and foreign objects (pieces of wood or bone from the dog's chewing habits).

✔ Pay attention to tartar as it can bring on gum disease and tooth decay. It also makes the dog's mouth look unsightly.

✔ Start very early with the Amstaff or APBT puppy to clean his teeth. As with so many other areas of dog ownership, the earlier you start it, the easier it will be!

✔ To clean your pet's teeth, use veterinarian-approved brushes and utensils and a toothpaste designed for dogs, not humans! Canine teeth cleaning is not difficult if you can get the pet

to come to enjoy or accept it early. Teeth cleaning will also largely involve brushing if you begin the practice with a puppy and continue it often and regularly. Two or three times a week is good; daily brushing is even better.

✔ Tartar scraping is never pleasant and comes as a result of neglecting your dog's teeth. This severe tartar removal may have to be done by the veterinarian.

✔ Schedule regular veterinary dental checkups with occasional professional teeth cleaning to catch any areas you may have missed.

✔ Use veterinarian-approved and experienced Amstaff/APBT breeder-reviewed chew toys and dental exercisers to help in keeping tartar at a minimum.

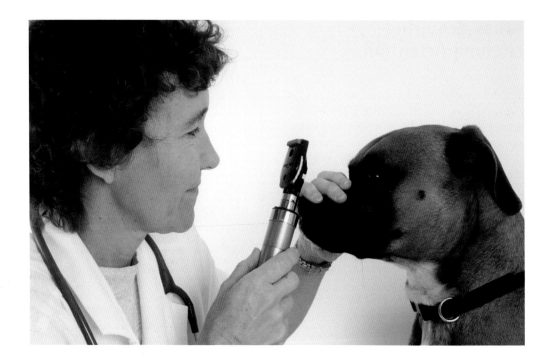

✔ The only adequate way to clean your pet's teeth is through regular care by you and regular cleaning by a professional. Dog biscuits and chew toys are no substitute for good home care and professional attention.

## Eyes

Your American Pit Bull Terrier or American Staffordshire Terrier does not have the large prominent eyes of some breeds. This does not mean that these dogs will be immune to eye injuries or eye problems. Often, dogs of these breeds are very exuberant and active. Such love of life can cause a pet to not notice possible eye-injuring situations. As the pet owner, it will be your job to help prevent these injuries. There are several ways to do this:

**1.** In places where your pet is allowed to play or run, be alert for sharp pointed things the dog might not see such as thorns, briars, barbed wire, stems, and rosebushes (especially those that may have been recently trimmed and are just at a dog's eye level).

**2.** Caution children about throwing stones, playing with air rifles, and other activities that could be injurious to a curious pet's eyes.

**3.** Keep your pet from chemical harm to his eyes by avoiding places where considerable air pollution is taking place or where recent or residual chemical spraying could be on grass or shrubs and get into your pet's eyes.

**4.** Do not let your pet ride with his head out of an automobile window.

**5.** Check your dog's eyes each day for injuries, foreign matter, reddening, or infection. You may notice that mucus sometimes appears in the corners of your American Staffordshire's or APBT's eyes. Normally, this is perfectly natural and can simply be removed gently with a soft cloth. This mucus should not be confused with a discharge that should get veterinary attention.

## Ears

Your American Pit Bull Terrier or American Staffordshire Terrier can have either cropped or uncropped (natural) ears. Cropped or uncropped ears will still need daily inspection for injuries, infection, or infestations of ear mites (see page 84) or ticks (see page 83). Pay attention to the inside and outside of your dog's ears.

## Feet and Toenails

Your American Pit Bull Terrier or American Staffordshire Terrier usually has sturdy feet, well able to support a solid medium-sized dog. However, every dog can sometimes have foot troubles.

**City:** City living poses particular hazards. Running over paved surfaces can keep the toenails worn down where they may not need much trimming. However, city-dwelling APBTs and Amstaffs will suffer more damage to the pads of their feet from the rough, unyielding surfaces of concrete, paving stone, and asphalt. Bruises and abrasions are more often seen in this environment. Salt on winter sidewalks can also irritate a dog's feet.

**Rural:** The rural APBT or Amstaff won't miss out on foot concerns either. Constantly walking or running in a grassy backyard will not wear down nails and these will grow too long unless you trim them. Splinters, thorns, slivers of

broken glass, and even small stones can get between a pet's toes or in the soft tissue of the pad and cause trouble.

Daily inspections of your dog's feet will prevent most minor conditions from becoming major problems. Trimming your dog's toenails, like brushing his teeth, must be started early to be easily accomplished. You need a good set of

canine nail clippers, which can be either the scissors type or the guillotine type. As your dog's nails grow, trim back just the tips on each nail. Don't cut too deeply or the quick, or blood supply to the nail, will be injured and may bleed. Following trimming, smooth the edges of the nail with a nail file or an emery board.

# Administering Medicine

You should know how to administer the prescriptions your veterinarian gives you to keep your pet healthy or help him regain his health. This activity is not always as easy as it sounds. Like a lot of American Pit Bull Terrier or American Staffordshire Terrier care, it should be started while the animal is still a puppy.

Some dogs just do not like to be dosed with medicine. They will spit out capsules or tablets. Some dog owners will hide a pill in a treat in order to get it down.

A more direct approach and one that can be used when a dog may catch on to the treat trick is to:

✔ Speak calmly and reassuringly as you open the dog's mouth.

✔ Tilt his head back only slightly. Place the pill as far back on the dog's tongue as possible (or in the case of liquid medicine, pour it over the back of the tongue).

✔ Gently but firmly close the dog's mouth, holding the jaws closed with your hand, and continue to talk to the dog until he swallows the medicine.

✔ Always remember to follow the veterinarian's instructions, dosages, and medication schedule carefully. Never give your American Pit Bull Terrier or Amstaff human medicines or remedies without your veterinarian's prior approval.

# When Your APBT/Amstaff Grows Older

These breeds have a good, long life span and may be with you and your family well into their teens. Gradually that humorous, innocent puppy that became that powerful American Pit Bull Terrier or American Staffordshire Terrier will turn into a gray-muzzled senior. Normally, a dog of these breeds will age well and keep both his good health and his devotion to his humans.

The oldster will sleep a little more, play a little less. He will still want to be included in family activities and not be replaced by a younger and more vigorous puppy. All of the teeth, eyes, ears, feet, and toenail care areas take on added importance with a distinguished veteran. Your visits to the veterinarian may come a little more often as your pet's health needs change.

You will need to be certain that the dog is fed a good senior dog food that will not contribute to obesity, a condition that will really harm an older pet. Your pet may need a little less food and a few more frequent walks and visits to the relief spot.

All in all, the magic of the American Pit Bull Terrier or the American Staffordshire Terrier will still be there. Slower, more willing to watch than participate, but still desperately in need of your loving touch and approval, your older pet will still have as much affection for you and

your family as he ever had. You will need to be sure that your old dog knows that you still love him too.

## Saying Good-bye (Euthanasia)

That inquisitive, little Amstaff or APBT that won your heart at the breeder's will make way for the frisky adolescent and then the sturdy adult. Over the years, this American Staffordshire or American Pit Bull Terrier will have become a trusted and greatly loved member of your family.

One day your APBT/Amstaff may begin a downward slide in health and activity. Under ideal circumstances, your pet would be relatively healthy one day and then quietly and painlessly die in his sleep that night.

In most cases, though, barring fatal accidents or injuries, an old dog will just grow older and older until age and infirmity make his existence one of pain and anguish. It is at this point that the hardest decision a pet owner will ever have to make must be made.

When the life of your loving American Staffordshire or American Pit Bull Terrier becomes void of the fun of former times and when the dog looks to you with imploring eyes for an explanation for all the pain and physical incapacity, your decision must be one based on the best interests of the dog. Your veterinarian, now hopefully an old friend to both you and your Amstaff or APBT, can be consulted. Euthanasia will be a gentle end to a full and happy life that has taken on very painful aspects. Ultimately, the decision is yours and it will never be easy. However, there comes a time when you grasp all the positive memories and hold them tight and say good-bye to a dear and devoted friend.

## Organizations

The American Kennel Club (AKC)
5580 Centerview Drive
Raleigh, NC 27606-3390
*www.akc.org*

United Kennel Club
100 E. Kilgore Road
Kalamazoo, MI 49002-5584
*www.ukcdogs.com*

Canadian Kennel Club
89 Skyway Avenue, Suite 100
Etobicoke, Ontario M9W 6R4
*www.ckc.ca*

The Kennel Club
1 Clarges Street
London W1J 8AB
*www.thekennelclub.org.uk*

American Dog Breeders Association (ADBA)
*(strictly American Pit Bull Terriers)*
P.O. Box 1771
Salt Lake City, UT 84110
(801) 936-7513

National American Pit Bull Terrier Association
210 East Walnut North
Baltimore, MD 45872
*www.napbt.com*

Staffordshire Terrier Club of America
11781 Arguello Drive
Mira Loma, CA 91752-3039
*www.amstaff.org*

## Books

Favorito, F., *American Pit Bull Terrier,* Freehold, New Jersey: Kennel Club Books (A Division of Bow Tie, Inc), 2007.

Gewirtz, Elaine, *American Pit Bull Terriers* (Animal Planet Series) Neptune City, New Jersey: T.F.H. Publications, 2006.

Jessup, Diane, *The Working Pit Bull,* Neptune City, New Jersey: T.F.H. Publications, 1995.

Millan, Cesar, *Be the Pack Leader: Use Cesar's Way to Transform Your Dog... and Your Life,* Harmony Books (Crown Publishing), 2007.

___. *A Member of the Family: Cesar Millan's Guide to a Lifetime of Fulfillment with Your Dog,* Harmony Books (Crown Publishing), 2008.

Nicholas, Anna Katherine, *American Staffordshire Terriers,* Neptune City, New Jersey: T.F.H. Publications, 1997.

Stahlkuppe, Joe, *The American Pit Bull Terrier Handbook,* Hauppauge, New York: Barron's Educational Series, Inc., 2000.

Stahlkuppe, Joe, *Training Your Pit Bull,* Hauppauge, New York: Barron's Educational Series, Inc., 2006.

## Rescue/Adoption Organizations

Pit Bull Rescue Central (PBRC)
(Clearinghouse for Amstaffs/APBTs and mixes in shelters and for adoption)
*pbrc.net*

Staffordshire Club of America—
    Rescue Committee
*rescue@amstaff.org*

adjustment to new home, 32–34
adopting an APBT/Amstaff,
    17–19, 21–27
aggressive behavior, 49
allergies, 80–81

body language, 43
buying a dog, 21–27

cages, 26–27, 34–37
caring for APBT/Amstaff, 49–53
characteristics, 41–42
children and APBT/Amstaff,
    42–43
collars and leashes, 26
commands, 63–69
crates and crate training, 26–27,
    34–37, 58–60

death, 91
diseases, 75–84
documents, 22–23
dog fighting, 6–8

ears, 89
emergency care, 85–86
equipment, 63
euthanasia, 91
exercise, 50
expectations prior to
    buying/adopting, 21–24
eyes, 88–89

feet, 89
fenced yards, 27, 49
fleas, 83
food and feeding, 25, 38, 51–52

grooming, 50–51
guarantees, health and
    temperament, 23

health care, 72–91
health records, 22–23

hip dysplasia, 23, 79–80
history, 5–9
housetraining, 52–53, 70–71

illnesses, 75–86
immunizations, 74–75
inherited conditions, 81

leashes, 26

misperceptions about, 5–9
mother dog's training model,
    57–58

neighborhood relations, 46
neuter/spay agreements, 23–24

obedience classes, 69
older APBT/Amstaff, 91
organizations, 92
other dogs, 44
other pets, 45
overbreeding, 6–8
owner responsibilities, 11–12

pack behavior, 56–57
parasites, 81–83
play, 36
poisons, 86–87
prevention, 74
puppies, 28–29, 60–71

registration papers, 22
resources, 92
return policy, 24

safety for children, 42–43
selecting an APBT/Amstaff, 24–25
shelter dogs, 17–19, 21, 25
skin problems, 80–81
socialization, 24–25, 31–33
spay/neuter agreements, 23–24
strangers and APBT/Amstaff,
    45–46

teeth, 87–88
temperament guarantees, 23
ticks, 83–84
toenails, 89–90
toothbrushes, 26
toys, 26
training, 49–53, 52–53, 55–71

vomiting, 79

walking your APBT/Amstaff, 49
worms, 81–83

**Important Note**

This guide tells the reader how to care for an American Pit Bull Terrier and an American Staffordshire Terrier. The advice given primarily concerns normally developed puppies from a good breeder in excellent physical condition and of good character.

Anyone who adopts a fully grown dog should be aware that the animal has already formed his basic impression of human beings. The new owner should watch the animal carefully, including his behavior toward humans, and should meet the previous owner.

Caution is further advised in the association of children with dogs, in meeting with other dogs, and in exercising the dog without a leash.

Even well-behaved and carefully supervised dogs can sometimes damage someone else's property or cause accidents. It is in the owner's interest to be adequately insured against such eventualities. We strongly urge all dog owners to purchase a liability policy that covers their dogs.